STRATEGIC PLANNING SIMPLIFIED

THE CLARITY METHOD: A REFRESHINGLY SIMPLE, FLEXIBLE, AND PRACTICAL APPROACH DESIGNED FOR NON-PROFIT ORGANIZATIONS

MELISSA HAFFEMAN

HAFF NOTES

Haffeman Productions

Copyright

© 2025 Melissa Haffeman

All rights reserved.

This publication is intended to provide general guidance and practical tools for strategic planning. It is not a substitute for legal, financial, or professional advice. Readers are encouraged to consult qualified professionals regarding specific decisions or circumstances.

Every effort has been made to ensure the accuracy and reliability of the information at the time of publication. The author and publisher assume no liability for how this material is used.

Want to go deeper?

Explore courses, guides, consulting, and practical tools for your next step at: www.melissahaffeman.com

For permissions, inquiries, or bulk orders, please contact: hello@haffeman.com

ISBNs:

(EPUB): 979-8-9883158-6-5

(Print): 979-8-9883158-7-2

Haffeman Productions LLC

Library of Congress Control Number: 2025911142

Printed in the United States of America

First Edition

This book is dedicated to Mike, Sophia, and Alden for contributing so many morning discussions exploring ideas with a cup of coffee or hot cocoa in hand.

CONTENTS

A NEW WAY TO PLAN

P icture this: You walk into your non-profit's strategic planning meeting feeling steady and prepared. You've gathered input from stakeholders and organized their thoughts into coherent goals. You know where the group agrees and disagrees. And instead of starting from scratch or trying to wrangle a dozen competing opinions, you have a clear process in front of you—one that actually works.

The conversation feels focused and respectful. People are engaged. Decisions are being made. And you're not just checking a box—you're building something together.

This is what strategic planning can look like.

But for many people, it hasn't felt that way. Maybe you've experienced the opposite: multi-day retreats with giant sticky notes, strong voices dominating the conversation, and a vague document that no one looks at again. You're not alone if that's what comes to mind.

The good news? It doesn't have to be that way.

If you're holding this book, there's a good chance you've been asked to "lead the strategic plan." Maybe you're the executive director, the board president, a program director—or the person others naturally turn to when something important needs doing. You want this to go well, but you're not exactly sure what that looks like.

That's okay. You don't need to be a strategic planning expert. You just need a method that makes sense—and that's exactly what this book offers.

This is *Strategic Planning Simplified: The Clarity Method*—a refreshingly simple, flexible, and practical approach designed for real-world teams. It helps you involve the stakeholders at the right level, guide the discussions so they don't get mired in minutia, and walk away with a one-page plan your team can actually use.

This method is for the facilitator. Whether you're stepping into this role for the first time or looking for a better way to do it, this approach gives you a clear framework and the tools to guide your group with confidence.

Here's what you can expect:

- You'll gather meaningful input before the meeting ever begins.
- You'll walk into the room with clarity about what matters most.
- You'll guide your team toward thoughtful, aligned decisions—without burnout.

This isn't about moving through the strategic planning motions so your organization can say it's done it. It's about creating a space where people feel heard, where their ideas are visible, and where decisions actually lead to action. When the prep is thoughtful and the process is grounded, something shifts. People show up differently. The conversation deepens. And the outcome is a plan that feels both ambitious and achievable.

I created the Strategic Planning Simplified: Clarity Method because I needed it. Over the last 20 years, I've worked in schools, nonprofits, and small businesses. I've been a principal, a founder, a board member, and a business and strategy coach. I've seen what happens when strategic planning is done well—and what happens when it's not.

I've been in those long meetings that led nowhere. I've watched good intentions get buried under too much discussion that goes in circles. And I've walked alongside leaders who knew things had to change but didn't know how to bring people along.

So I built a different approach.

It's not flashy. But it works. It's practical, flexible, and designed for real-world teams with real-world constraints. It honors people's time and wisdom. And it helps you create a strategic plan that people actually believe in.

This process has been used in schools, nonprofits, and small businesses. It works because it respects people's time and insights. It simplifies the planning process without watering it down. And it results in a one-page plan that actually gets used.

That plan won't sit in a drawer. It'll show up in board meetings, team check-ins, and big-picture decisions. It'll remind you what matters most, and how to stay focused when things get busy.

This process is yours now. Use it. Adapt it. Make it fit your world. But most of all, trust yourself. You don't have to have all the answers. You just need to take the first step—and be willing to guide the group with clarity and care.

You're more ready than you think.

Let's get started.

2

WHERE IT ALL STARTS

You've been asked to lead strategic planning for your nonprofit. Maybe you're a board secretary, a staff leader, or the person who didn't step back fast enough in the last meeting. Regardless, the task is now yours.

If you're thinking, "Me? I'm not qualified for this," you're not alone. Most people don't feel prepared to lead strategic planning. But here's the truth: with the right structure and tools, you can do this—and it's my goal to help you enjoy the process along the way.

This chapter walks you through the essential steps of the process, gives you a sense of what success looks like, and helps you determine if your organization is ready.

Start with Readiness

Before you start planning, ask: Is the organization ready? This method works best when your nonprofit has a basic level of stability and relationships are respectful. You don't need perfect harmony—just a willingness to show up and work toward a shared goal.

You're likely ready if:

- Your board and staff generally collaborate well
- There's shared understanding of the mission
- Key stakeholders are willing to participate
- Someone can serve as facilitator (maybe that's you)
- The organization has been active for 1–2 years or more

You're definitely ready if:

- There's disagreement about priorities—but it stays respectful
- Some board members are new and want clarity
- Your last strategic plan expired (or never existed)
- Stakeholders want more involvement
- You want everyone to feel heard in the process

When You Might Need Outside Help

Most groups can lead this process themselves using the tools in this book. But in some cases, a professional facilitator helps:

- Major change (mergers, new leadership, big shifts)
- Deep tension or lack of trust
- Exploring radically new territory

Even then, you can use this process to lay the groundwork. It helps everyone show up informed and ready, whether or not you bring in a consultant.

The Facilitator's Toolkit

You're not building the whole plan on your own—you're equipping others to build it as well-collaboratively. Think of yourself as holding a well-organized toolkit. Each compartment contains the tools your group will need: vision, input, priorities, a meeting framework, and a simple final plan.

Overview of the Strategic Planning: Clarity Method

Strategic Planning Simplified:
The 5-Part Clarity Method

STRATEGIC PLAN

STRATEGIC
PLANNING MEETING

PRIORITY SORT

STAKEHOLDER
SURVEY

EXECUTIVE
BRIEF

- **Vision**: You start by capturing where your organization is today—a clear, honest snapshot that becomes your executive brief.

- **Input**: You send that brief to stakeholders and ask three key questions. Their answers come back as thoughtful insights, not heat-of-the-moment reactions.
- **Priorities**: You take the collected input and sort it. Stakeholders help determine what matters most—before the meeting even starts.
- **Meeting**: You gather. But instead of starting from scratch, you begin with a draft plan. This makes it easier to refine, align, and decide.
- **Plan**: You leave with a one-page roadmap. Clear goals, assigned responsibilities, and a rhythm for follow-through.

Your role is not to have all the answers. It's to bring the right tools and create the right structure so your team can build something great—together.

This process works because it removes the chaos. It gives people time to reflect instead of react. It honors the quiet voices. It keeps the loud ones in check. And it leads to a plan people actually understand and want to follow.

You don't have to be an expert. You just have to trust the process, prepare well, and lead with clarity.

———————————

Action Steps

If your organization meets the readiness criteria above:

- Commit to being the facilitator, even if you're learning as you go
- Talk with your board chair or ED to confirm alignment on the process using this method
- Block out 6–8 weeks to follow the planning steps described in this book
- Create a shared folder to keep documents organized

If your organization is on the fence:

- Start by reviewing the readiness checklist with a trusted colleague
- Use the Appendix template "Facilitator Readiness Worksheet" to talk through potential challenges and strengths

Chapter Review

- This framework flips the traditional planning process
- You start with readiness, then move through clear steps
- Input is gathered early, meetings are efficient, and outcomes are actionable

3

ALEX'S STORY: BRIGHTSTART READERS

To bring this strategic planning process to life, we'll be following the story of a fictional nonprofit organization: BrightStart Readers—and its relatively new Executive Director, Alexandra Morgan.

Alex's story represents what many nonprofit leaders experience: limited time, passionate people, high expectations, and a desire to make real progress. As you move through the chapters ahead, you'll see how Alex uses the process in this book to guide her team through a clear and inclusive strategic planning effort. But first, let's take a few minutes to get to know this fictional non-profit organization.

About the Organization: BrightStart Readers

Vision: A future where every child reads confidently by third grade.

Mission: BrightStart Readers is committed to increasing literacy rates by providing free one-on-one reading mentorship and access to books for elementary students in under-resourced communities.

Values:

- Equity in education
- Joy in learning
- Empowerment through literacy
- Community-rooted support
- Accountability to those we serve

Organizational Snapshot:

- **Founded**: approximately 29 years ago
- **Annual Budget**: $275,000
- **Staff**: 3 full-time, 2 part-time
- **Volunteers**: ~60 active reading mentors
- **Board**: 9 members
- **Board Meetings**: Monthly, with one annual stakeholder meeting

Board Profiles:

- **Shannon (Board Chair)** – A retired elementary principal, passionate about literacy but tends to dominate conversations
- **Sean** – A local librarian, highly knowledgeable but often quiet in meetings
- **Karen** – Parent of a former program participant, brings the family perspective
- **Maya** – New board member, works in corporate HR, analytical and eager to help
- **Tom** – Treasurer, CPA, focused on fiscal responsibility

- **Luis, Erin, Sasha and Ben** – Rounding out the board with a mix of community outreach, fundraising, and nonprofit experience

BrightStart Readers has made an impact in the community but never had a formal strategic plan. Alex knows this is the right time.

About Alexandra Morgan

Alex stepped into her role as Executive Director just nine months ago. Previously, she served as the volunteer coordinator for a regional literacy nonprofit. She's driven, empathetic, and highly organized—but new to leading a board-driven planning process. She was handed the responsibility of leading strategic planning during her second board meeting. She said yes—partly out of enthusiasm, partly out of panic.

Alex's goals are simple: to create a plan that reflects the heart of the organization, involves all voices, and actually helps them grow. She's also looking for clarity on what she should be focused on in her job. She wants the board to feel invested, the staff to feel heard, and the plan to be something they revisit often—not just a document on a shelf.

In the chapters ahead, you'll walk alongside Alex and her team as they:

- Create their first executive brief
- Design and launch a stakeholder input process
- Analyze and sort priorities
- Facilitate a planning meeting
- Finalize and implement their one-page plan

As you move through the chapters ahead, you'll follow the process alongside Alex. Her story gives you a front-row seat to what this looks like in action—what decisions feel like, what challenges might arise, and how each step builds momentum. You'll be able to see the tools in use and adapt them for your own organization.

4

YOUR ROLE AS THE FACILITATOR

Let's take a quick trip back to school for a moment. Remember those infamous group projects? The ones where one person did 95% of the work while everyone else just showed up, nodded, and somehow still got an A?

Let's be really clear: this is *not* that.

Strategic planning isn't about you carrying the whole thing or quietly doing all the work behind the scenes. And it's definitely not about showing up with a finished product and hoping everyone signs off.

In this process, you're something entirely different.

You're not the overachiever doing it all. You're not the teacher giving out grades.

You're the one with the whiteboard saying:

"Okay, we've got a plan. Let's divide and conquer. Everyone's voice matters—and we're going to make this work together."

You're the **facilitator**.

What a Great Facilitator *Actually* Does

Let's make this tangible. A strong facilitator isn't just leading a single meeting—they're guiding the entire planning journey. From the first conversation to the final plan, you're creating structure, focus, and flow.

Throughout the process, you'll:

- **Keep the group grounded** in the bigger picture— what this process is for and why it matters
- **Keep things on track,** so each phase (survey, sort, meeting, final plan) builds on the last
- **Nudge the conversation**, gently steering the group when the conversation dives into the details instead of staying on the big picture
- **Make space for quieter voices**, so insights don't get lost in the noise
- **Hold the timeline**, helping the group move forward without feeling rushed
- **Summarize agreements** clearly so people know what's been decided—and what's still open
- **Visually track the work**, projecting the plan framework or writing decisions in real time so progress is visible
- **Step back when needed**, letting the group lead while still guiding the process forward
- **Bring steady energy**, especially when the team feels stuck, uncertain, or tired.

You don't have to be the loudest or most experienced person in the room. You just have to keep showing up with clarity, care, and a steady hand on the process.

What If You're Also the ED or a Board Member?

Now, this part's important. A lot of facilitators are also executive directors or board members—which means you're not just running the meeting, you're also part of the group being affected by the outcome.

And yes, that can feel a little awkward.

You care deeply about the direction of the organization. You probably have strong ideas about what should happen next. But your greatest power in this process isn't pushing your own vision—it's building one the whole group believes in.

That doesn't mean you can't participate. You should absolutely fill out the stakeholder survey. You can share ideas and advocate for your goals. But when it comes time to facilitate the conversation, your primary role is holding space—not steering it. The key is to strike that balance between organization member and facilitator.

A facilitator who leads with neutrality builds trust. And trust? That's what allows people to show up fully and take ownership of the final plan.

Think: Potluck, Not Performance

Still feeling a little unsure? Let's go to a food metaphor.

If strategic planning is like preparing a big community meal, you're not the chef doing it all alone. And you're definitely not a food critic judging everyone's dish.

You're the potluck organizer:

- Making sure there's a place for everyone at the table
- Checking that someone brought main dishes—not just seven desserts
- Noticing if someone's feeling left out
- Gently inviting the quiet folks to share what they brought

Your job isn't to wow anyone with your vision.

Your job is to help the group co-create something meaningful —something they'll actually eat, enjoy, and remember.

Why This Matters

Facilitation isn't flashy. But it's powerful.

When a group feels like their ideas matter... When they can see the plan forming in real time... When no one person is dominating the space...

That's when planning stops feeling like a chore—and starts becoming a shared mission.

That's when the real magic happens.

And the best part? You don't have to be a polished speaker or a professional consultant to do this well. You just have to be steady, thoughtful, and clear about your role.

Action Steps

- Clarify your role as facilitator—not the expert, not the decision-maker, but the guide

- Reflect on where you'll need to show up most: structure, pacing, listening, or redirecting
- If you're also the ED or a board member, decide when you'll participate and when you'll hold space
- Practice describing your role to others using language like:"I'm here to guide the process, not push a specific plan."
- Bookmark or print this chapter as a touchstone throughout your process

Chapter Review

- Your role as facilitator is to guide the *entire process*, not just the planning meeting
- Great facilitation means keeping the process clear, inclusive, and on track
- Neutrality—especially when you're also a team member—builds trust and deepens participation
- A well-lead process creates space for better conversations, stronger decisions, and shared ownership

5

WHO'S INVOLVED

Before you begin building the plan, you need to decide who will help build it with you.

In your facilitator role, this is one of your first and most important responsibilities: choosing the right people to hold the tools and shape the work. And just like any good build, you want the right crew—people who bring different strengths, perspectives, and steady hands.

Let's break it down.

Two Levels of Participation

In this method, we start wide and then go deep.

Level One is the input phase. This is where you invite as many stakeholders as possible to complete a brief survey. You'll gather ideas, hear concerns, and begin to understand what people hope for your organization's future.

Level Two is the core planning group. These are the folks who read that input, sort the priorities, and build the actual strategic plan together.

The survey gives you the raw materials. The planning group decides how to use them.

This two-part structure allows more people to be included while keeping the planning process focused and productive.

Who Should Participate Through the Survey

Not everyone needs to be part of the meeting where decisions are made. In fact, many people are better included in level one—through the stakeholder input survey.

Your level one group might include:

- Volunteers or staff who cannot commit to the full process
- Community members or past clients with valuable insight
- Partner organizations whose perspective can shape strategy
- Donors or more informal members of the organization

...and would definitely include:

- Everyone in the core group
- Your input as a member of the organization

These stakeholders help connect the dots. They share context —what's been tried, what's been talked about, and what people care about most. They help spot patterns you might not see from the inside. And sometimes, they're the first to surface emerging needs or new priorities before they become urgent.

It's not just about getting more opinions. It's about hearing from people who can help you understand what's underneath the surface—and what's coming next.

Who Should Be in the Core Group?

Every board member should be invited to join the core planning team.

Even if they're brand new or still learning the ropes, strategic planning is part of their governance role. Their participation gives the process legitimacy and ensures alignment with your organization's mission and responsibilities.

Here's who else to include:

- **Executive Director (or equivalent)** Their daily insight into operations and strategy is essential. If you're the ED, you're probably also the facilitator. That's fine—just be clear about when you're guiding the process and when you're offering your own ideas.
- **Key senior staff** If you have staff leads for programming, development, or operations, they should be part of this conversation. They'll be critical for implementation later on, and their input now prevents misalignment down the road.

Think of this group as your primary crew. They are the ones

who will handle the tools, take measurements, and help construct something real.

Who You Might Also Invite:

Depending on your organization's structure and mission, you may choose to add:

- **Long-time volunteers** with deep institutional memory
- **Major funders or donors** who understand your work and want to support it meaningfully
- **Community partners or service recipients** if your mission is rooted in place or equity

Ask yourself: Will this person help us build wisely? Will they bring a perspective that could shape how we prioritize and implement our goals?

If the answer is yes, and they're committed to showing up, they may be a good addition.

What This Might Look Like

Here are a few examples of how core planning teams typically come together:

Small Organization (3 to 8 people)

- Executive Director
- All board members or a board sub-group
- One or two key volunteers or senior staff

Midsize Organization (6 to 12 people)

- Executive Director and program lead
- Full board or selected board committee
- Long-serving volunteers or community partners

Larger Organization (8 to 15 people)

- Executive Director and senior leadership
- Board leadership and active board members
- A few trusted external voices (donors, partners, etc.)

There's no one right structure—but you'll know you've chosen well when the group feels balanced, invested, and capable of moving forward together.

Action Steps

- List all current board members and invite them to the core planning group
- Identify key staff, volunteers, or partners who need to be in the room as the core planning group
- Make a separate list of people who should complete the stakeholder survey
- Clarify expectations with anyone whose role or availability is uncertain
- Begin drafting your survey distribution list

Chapter Review

- Strategic planning works best when more people are invited into the process—but not everyone needs to make final decisions
- Level one (survey group) brings ideas, context, and early signals about emerging needs
- Level two (core group) builds the plan, based on what matters most
- Including all board members in the core group increases alignment and shared ownership
- Choosing participants with care keeps the process focused, inclusive, and productive

6

WHEN TO START

One of the most useful things you can do early in your facilitator role is help the group choose a timeline that is both realistic and steady. Not rushed. Not endless. Just clear enough to keep momentum, and spacious enough for people to think.

This step might seem small, but it sets the tone for everything that follows. If the timeline is too tight, people feel overwhelmed. If it's too vague, they lose energy. Either way, the plan gets harder to finish.

You don't need a perfect schedule. You just need one your group can follow and that fits your organization.

Start with the Finish Line—Then Check for Alignment

Start by choosing your strategic planning meeting date. That date becomes your anchor. Everything else—your survey, your sort, your prep time—gets scheduled by working backward from that point.

There are three recommended pacing options for this process: one month, two months, or three months. Each uses the same tools—you're simply adjusting the timeline to fit your organization's needs and availability.

But before you go too far with timelines or invitations, make sure you've had a quick check-in with the **board president** and the **executive director**.

If you are one of those people, you can make the decision directly. But if you're not, don't skip this step.

Take time to ask:

- Are there key deadlines or seasonal pressures we should account for?
- Are we expecting any major transitions that would affect planning?
- Does this timeline feel reasonable given everything else on the calendar?

This doesn't have to be a formal meeting. A short phone call or a thoughtful email will do. What matters is that the people responsible for governance and operations are aligned with your plan and understand what you're proposing.

You might say:

"I'm leaning toward a six-week timeline that ends with a planning session in mid-April. That gives us space to gather stakeholder input and prepare well. Does that feel workable to you?"

Getting their agreement now gives you the confidence—and permission—to move forward. It also gives you cover if unexpected delays pop up later. When leadership is on board with the pace, the process flows more easily.

Three Timeline Options

Let's look at three solid options. Each one uses the same tools —you're just adjusting the pace.

Option 1: Three-Month Timeline (Comprehensive)

This gives you the most breathing room and is great when you need more time for reflection or stakeholder engagement.

Month 1:

- Draft the executive brief
- Send the overview email and stakeholder survey
- Monitor responses and send reminders

Month 2:

- Analyze survey responses and key themes
- Build and send the priority sort
- Draft a sample agenda and working plan

Month 3:

- Facilitate the strategic planning meeting
- Draft and share the one-page plan
- Gather feedback and finalize
- Schedule quarterly follow-ups

Best for: organizations with multiple stakeholders, recent transitions, or complex dynamics

---

Option 2: Two-Month Timeline (Balanced)

This is the most common choice. It gives you time to do things well without stretching the process too far.

Month 1:

- Write and send your executive brief and stakeholder surveyBegin reading responses and identifying themes

Month 2:

- Send the priority sort
- Prepare the meeting agenda and packets
- Host your planning session
- Finalize the plan and schedule next steps

Best for: most small and midsize organizations with stable leadership

---

Option 3: One-Month Timeline (Intensive)

This one moves fast but can work well for small, nimble teams or those with a tight deadline.

Week 1:

- Draft and share your executive brief
- Launch the stakeholder survey

Week 2:

- Send reminders
- Analyze responses and build the sort

Week 3:

- Launch the sort
- Draft the plan framework and prep materials

Week 4:

- Facilitate your planning session
- Finalize and share the one-page plan

Best for: small teams, urgent needs, or organizations already aligned

---

How to Choose the Right Pace

Ask yourself:

- When do we need this plan completed?
- How much time do stakeholders realistically have?

- Do we need extra time for trust-building or board transitions?
- Are we trying to move quickly because of urgency, or because we're avoiding complexity?

Choose the pace your group can actually sustain. There's no bonus for rushing. And no shame in slowing down if it gets you to the finish line with clarity and support.

Communicate the Timeline Early

Once you've made your decision and checked in with leadership, communicate the timeline to everyone who will participate.

This can be a short message, a bullet-point email, or a calendar invite with a few lines of context. The goal is simply to set expectations and help people feel ready.

You might write to the core planning group:

"We'll be completing our strategic planning over the next six weeks. You'll receive a short survey next week, followed by a priority-setting activity. Then we'll meet to finalize the plan together. Thanks in advance for contributing your voice."

When people know what's coming, they're more likely to show up prepared—and more likely to follow through.

Action Steps

- Choose your strategic planning meeting date and anchor your schedule around it
- Select a timeline (1, 2, or 3 months) that fits your organization's needs
- Confirm your proposed pace with your board president and/or executive director
- Work backward from the meeting date to schedule each step of the process
- Share the full timeline with participants so expectations are clear from the beginning

Chapter Review

- A clear, steady timeline sets the tone for your entire planning process
- Working backward from your planning meeting helps you stay focused and realistic
- Leadership alignment is key—confirming the pace early saves confusion later
- Choose the pace your team can sustain; don't rush unless it truly serves your goals
- Clear communication around timing builds trust, readiness, and follow-through

7

ALEX'S STORY: PLANNING

The board meeting had wrapped thirty minutes ago, but Alex was still sitting at the table, laptop open, scribbling notes into the margin of a legal pad. Shannon, the board chair, had just asked her to take the lead on strategic planning—something about how Alex was "naturally organized and good with people." It was meant as a compliment, but it left Alex feeling the weight of expectation settle in her chest like a stone.

Back in her office, she slipped off her coat, pushed aside a stack of donor thank-you cards, and reached for the bookshelf. Halfway down the row, tucked between old program reports, she spotted a familiar spine: *Strategic Planning Simplified: The Clarity Method*. She recognized the bright yellow post-it on the cover—it had belonged to her predecessor, who had marked a few key pages but never gotten around to starting the strategic planning process.

Alex flipped it open, scanning the introduction. "You don't

need to be a strategic planning expert," it said. "You just need a method that makes sense."

She exhaled slowly. Maybe this was the path forward.

Within an hour, she'd devoured the first few chapters and begun sketching out the steps on her whiteboard. She highlighted the major phases: gather input, sort priorities, hold the planning session, finalize the one-page plan. It was doable. More than that—it was actually kind of exciting.

She opened her calendar and looked two months ahead. Mid-May. That gave her about eight weeks to get through the process without rushing. Enough time to be thoughtful, not so much that people would lose interest.

She drafted a quick text to Shannon.

> Hi Shannon—Thanks again for the conversation earlier. I've been reviewing a facilitation method I think will work really well for us. It's called Strategic Planning Simplified: The Clarity Method. I'm suggesting a two-month timeline, with a planning session around the second week of May. That would give us time to gather stakeholder input, sort priorities, and prepare well. Does that sound reasonable to you? Happy to talk through it anytime. – Alex

Shannon replied later that afternoon.

> Sounds perfect. I'd suggest looping in a few past volunteers on the survey—folks like Janet and Mike who moved out of town but still care deeply about our work. Let me know what you need from me.

Encouraged, Alex opened a spreadsheet and started drafting her stakeholder lists. One tab for the wide net—her survey group. The other for the core planning team.

The survey group was easy: all current board members, staff, regular volunteers, and several community partners. She added Shannon's suggested names, too—those long-time supporters who weren't local anymore but still read every newsletter and donated each December.

The core group took more thought. All nine board members, of course. Then herself. She added their part-time program manager and development lead. Karen, the parent represen-tative, brought an important perspective. And Maya, though new, had already shown she could bring structure to a conversation without taking over. That made thirteen. Manageable.

She double-checked the balance—voices from operations, fundraising, programming, governance, and lived experience. A good mix.

The next morning, she sent Shannon the draft list and a simple plan summary. Shannon replied with a thumbs-up and a "Let's go for it."

Alex smiled. For the first time, this didn't feel like a daunting mystery. It felt like a process she could lead—one step at a time.

But as she sat back in her chair and looked over the growing to-do list on her whiteboard, a new thought surfaced.

The survey.

She was about to ask people—people who had been involved with BrightStart Readers for years, sometimes decades—to share what they thought mattered most. And she'd only been in the ED role for nine months.

What if she missed something important? What if the questions felt off? What if the survey surfaced concerns she wasn't ready to answer?

Alex glanced over at the filing cabinet in the corner. Somewhere in there were board minutes from ten years ago. Maybe more. The organization had been around for nearly 30 years, after all. She felt the weight of that history, heavy and humbling.

Still, she knew what to do next.

She pulled out a clean notebook and wrote at the top:

Executive Brief: Where We've Been. Where We Are. Where We Might Be Going.

Then she underlined it.

Time to dig in.

8

CRAFTING THE EXECUTIVE BRIEF

B efore you bring your team together to talk about the future, you need to know where you're starting from—and the story that got you here.

That's what this chapter is about. **It's the first real step in the strategic planning process: gathering the information that helps everyone begin on common ground.**

This isn't the glamorous part. There's no big kickoff, no color-coded sticky notes. Just you, digging into documents, reviewing key data, and pulling together a clear, honest snapshot of your organization as it stands today.

Think of it as laying the foundation. It doesn't have to be fancy—but it does need to be solid.

Because if you skip this step and jump straight into planning, here's what often happens in the middle of the meeting:

Someone says, "We've always done it this way."Someone else

replies, "That's not true."And just like that, you're no longer planning—you're debating what's real.

Taking the time to gather and organize the facts prevents that spiral. It gives your team a shared starting point. It helps you walk into the room grounded, confident, and prepared—and that changes everything.

Think of This Step Like a Discovery Phase

Your goal here is to gather evidence—not to make decisions yet. You're pulling together the pieces that tell the story of where your organization has been, how it's evolved, and where it currently stands.

You're not writing a case study. You're creating a short, clear briefing. Just the facts. Something that anyone on your team —even a brand-new board member—can pick up and quickly understand.

Here's what you're looking for:

- Past strategic plans (even if outdated or forgotten)
- Board meeting minutes or summaries of important past discussions
- Key organizational milestones (what's changed, what's stayed steady)
- Founding documents like your mission, vision, and values
- Key metrics that describe your current scope and capacity—budgets, staffing, volunteers, program reach, or any other core data that helps illustrate today's reality

This is your discovery phase. Just like a lawyer gathers evidence before making a case, you're collecting the proof points that will help your team have more focused, informed conversations.

What You're Building: The Executive Brief

The foundational document of this strategic planning process is your **Executive Brief**.

Executive briefs are commonly used in high-stakes environments—places where leaders need to walk into a room fully informed. Think of the briefing books prepared for heads of state or CEOs, with key facts laid out clearly so they can make smart, fast decisions.

In this process, your Executive Brief does the same kind of work. It brings your team up to speed. It ensures that when people sit down to plan, they're starting with shared context —not assumptions or vague memories.

Your Executive Brief is a one-page snapshot that captures the heart of your organization—your mission, vision, values, key metrics, and a short summary of the nonprofit's history and current state.

You'll use this brief throughout the entire planning process:

- Share it with **survey respondents**, so they can offer meaningful input
- Include it in the **planning packet** for your core team
- Reference it in your **facilitated meeting**And file it with your **final plan**, as part of the historical record

STRATEGIC PLANNING SIMPLIFIED 39

Executive briefs are often used to bring decision-makers up to speed quickly. In this case, it's more than a backgrounder. It's your clarity tool. It helps connect ideas to real data. It creates alignment. And it becomes part of your organization's memory—so future teams can look back and see exactly where this process began.

It may not feel flashy. But don't underestimate this step. Creating the Executive Brief is one of the most important things you'll do as a facilitator.

Why This Step Matters

You're not just checking a box. You're doing something most strategic planning processes skip—and it's one of the reasons this method actually works.

You're taking time to define reality before trying to change it.

Here's why it matters: Imagine you're in the planning meeting, and someone suggests a big new initiative. It sounds exciting—but how do you know if it belongs in the plan?

Now imagine someone responds:

"I think that goal directly supports our mission, and it moves the needle on one of the key data points from our Executive Brief. It addresses the challenge we identified around [fill in the blank], and it fits with where we've been headed for the last few years."

That's not just an opinion. That's a case. And people listen differently when something is backed by context.

This kind of clarity shifts the tone of the meeting. It grounds ambition. It invites honesty. It helps people bring new ideas without losing track of what already exists.

And when you walk into the planning meeting with this document in hand, it sends a quiet but powerful signal: **We're not starting from scratch. We're starting from here.**

You Don't Have to Do It Alone

This doesn't have to be your solo task. If you're not sure where to find something—like an old strategic plan or a set of program numbers—ask your board chair, your bookkeeper, your staff lead, or whoever holds the missing puzzle pieces.

You don't need to have all the information. You just need to be willing to collect it, organize it, and put it in one place.

That alone will set your process apart and level up the quality of strategic planning for your non-profit.

Action Steps

- Gather past strategic plans or planning materials (if any)
- Review meeting minutes for major themes and goals
- Understand your organization's founding story, mission, and vision
- Pull together key data—budgets, staff counts, program impact, etc.
- Create a clean, simple one-page Executive Brief that summarizes what you've found

Chapter Review

- Strategic planning begins with clarity—starting from a shared understanding
- The Executive Brief is your foundational tool for gathering and presenting that clarity
- This document brings context, alignment, and structure to every step of the process
- The Executive Brief needs to be one to two pages maximum. Ideally one page.

9

ALEX'S STORY: RESEARCH

The folder was almost an afterthought.

She found it while cleaning the corner shelf behind her office printer—a dusty pile labeled *Board Retreat—2016* in fading pen. Most of it was scribbled agendas and half-legible flip chart notes, full of half-finished goals and big ideas that had clearly never seen daylight again.

But to Alex, it felt like finding an old journal in someone else's handwriting.

There were ideas for expanding to three new schools. A draft mission statement revision. Even a scribbled note:

Create volunteer appreciation committee?

…complete with a coffee stain across the margin.

She smiled. Not because it was groundbreaking, but because someone, at some point, had *tried*.

Over the next few days, Alex became part historian, part detective.

She pulled the organization's original mission, vision, and values from the state's filing system. She scheduled coffee with two of the founders—retired now, but still proud of what they'd started. Their eyes lit up when they talked about the first reading sessions, the first donated book shelf, the first time a kid asked, "Can I keep this one?"

She chatted with Luis, one of the longest-serving volunteers, who remembered running story-time out of a community center basement. "We had two bins of books," he said, "and a lot of duct tape holding it all together."

She collected more than nostalgia. She pulled numbers: how many volunteers were active now, how many elementary schools were partnered, how many books had been handed out last year. She gathered three testimonials—from a fourth-grade student, a parent, and a teacher—each one quietly powerful in its own way.

And little by little, something clicked.

This wasn't just a fact-finding mission anymore. She was building something. A bridge between the past and the present. A document that told the truth of who BrightStart Readers was—and where they stood today.

She called it the Executive Brief.

It wasn't glamorous. Just one clean page: their mission, vision, values. Key data points. A short timeline of their story. A sentence or two about what mattered most right now.

But as Alex read it back, she felt something shift.

This wasn't just for the strategic planning meeting. It was for *her*. For every donor meeting where someone asked, "So what's your impact?" For every new board member who needed a starting point. For herself—on the hard days when everything felt like a blur of logistics and inboxes.

She wasn't guessing anymore. She *knew* the organization.

She emailed the brief to Shannon, the board chair, and paced while waiting. The response came within the hour:

"This is exactly what we needed. Clear, grounded, and real. Let's share it. Approved."

Alex exhaled. One big step was officially behind her.

But as she opened a new Google Doc—Stakeholder Survey – Draft—a familiar tension crept up her spine.

She'd taken surveys before. The kind that asked too much, said too little, or left her wondering why she bothered filling it out at all. She didn't want that. Not here. Not now.

She wanted questions that mattered. Prompts that drew out the gold. She wanted people to feel seen—and to actually *say* what they thought. But crafting those questions? She had no idea where to start.

Her fingers hovered over the keyboard.

One blinking cursor. One blank page.

And the entire voice of the organization waiting on the other side.

10

CRAFTING YOUR STRATEGIC PLANNING SURVEY

W elcome to the part of the process where you create one of the most powerful tools in your facilitator's toolbox: the strategic planning survey. This isn't your average feedback form. It's a thoughtfully designed conversation starter—one that invites every stakeholder to speak freely, reflect deeply, and influence the direction of your organization.

The beauty of this method is its ability to gather honest, grounded input without requiring people to show up to a four-hour meeting. You're building something more accessible, more inclusive, and—ultimately—more useful.

Why the Survey Matters

Let's be honest: strategic planning meetings can turn into a marathon of voices—some loud, some quiet, some missing altogether. People with the strongest opinions tend to dominate, while others hold back or disappear altogether.

The survey changes that.

It invites everyone into the conversation on equal footing. No microphone. No pressure. Just a few open-ended questions, thoughtfully answered.

You'll send this survey to both your core planning group and a broader set of stakeholders—your Level One participants (see Chapter 5). Their responses become the raw materials you'll use to sort priorities and build your plan.

Why Anonymity Is So Important

When people know their name isn't attached to their response, they speak more freely. They're more likely to be honest, more likely to share a difficult truth, and more likely to suggest bold ideas. Anonymity removes the pressure of group dynamics and lets people be real. It creates a safe space for truth to surface.

So yes—make your survey anonymous. Say it clearly in the instructions. And thank people for their candor.

Why Long-Form Responses Work

Long-form responses help you go deeper. They tell you *why* something matters, not just *what* someone thinks. A multiple-choice survey might tell you that five people think you should expand a program—but a long-form response will tell you what problem they're trying to solve, or what story moved them.

To get long responses, write prompts that feel like invitations, not tasks. Use phrases like:

- "We'd love your full thoughts on this."
- "Take your time—details are welcome."
- "What's been on your mind about this?"
- "In your own words..."

That tone matters. It makes people feel like their words will be heard—not just scanned.

Three Essential Questions

Your survey doesn't need to be long. In fact, shorter is better —as long as the questions are strong.

Here are the three recommended questions:

1. What's missing from our Executive Brief? Use this to validate your snapshot of the past and present. You might phrase it like:

"After reading the Executive Brief, is there anything you feel is missing or should be included before we move forward with planning?"

2. What are the top three priorities we should focus on over the next three years? This is the open door for ideas. People will use it to name what matters to them. Encourage detail:

"Please share the top three things you believe the organization should accomplish in the next three years. Detailed responses are appreciated."

3. What would success look and feel like three years from now? This is your curveball—the vision prompt. It forces optimism and imagination:

"If our organization were highly successful three years from now, what would people say about us? What would the experience be like for staff, clients, or community members?"

This question helps uncover the *why* behind their hopes and goals. It's gold.

Facilitator Note: You might be wondering, "Only three questions? Is that really enough?" It is—and here's why. This method is intentionally streamlined so people will actually respond. When questions are clear and open-ended, people go deeper. You get fuller, more thoughtful answers—and less survey fatigue. Plus, this is just the beginning. Their input will be sorted and shaped into a full discussion in your planning meeting. The magic isn't in asking *more*—it's in asking *better*. Trust it.

What Software Should I Use?

Good news: you don't need anything fancy. Here are a few survey tools that work beautifully for this:

- **Google Forms** – free, easy to use, and anonymous by default
- **SurveyMonkey** – simple design and great for small teams (free or paid)
- **Typeform** – beautiful, mobile-friendly forms that feel like conversations

All three options allow you to export responses easily for review and analysis.

Reading and Analyzing Responses

Yes, you'll need to read them. But you don't have to do it alone. AI tools like ChatGPT or Claude can help you summarize themes, pull quotes, and cluster priorities. But always do a first pass yourself. You'll see nuance, tone, and insight that a bot might miss. And when you quote someone directly in the planning meeting? That makes people feel seen.

Set Expectations

When you send your survey, be clear:

- It's anonymous
- It's short (3–5 questions max)
- It takes just 10–15 minutes
- Narrative responses are welcome, needed, and appreciated

Let people know you genuinely want to hear from them—and they'll rise to meet you.

Action Steps

- Choose 3–5 open-ended survey questions using the examples above
- Select your survey tool (Google Forms, SurveyMonkey, or Typeform)
- Set up the survey with anonymity enabled

- Review your Executive Brief to make sure your first question fits
- Draft the email you'll use to send the survey to both levels of your planning team

Chapter Review

- The strategic planning survey is the great equalizer—it invites honest input from every voice
- Anonymity builds trust and encourages real feedback
- Open-ended, narrative responses give you rich insight you can't get from checkboxes
- Short surveys (3–5 well-phrased questions) are more likely to be completed—and more useful

11

COMMUNICATING WITH CLARITY

You've done the quiet, foundational work—chosen who participates and at what level, mapped out your timeline, written your Executive Brief, and created the survey. Now it's time to bring people in.

This is where everything starts to take shape.

Here's the truth: people need to see or hear something *many* times before it sinks in. That's not a flaw—it's just how our brains work. Think about marketing. Repetition isn't annoying when it's done well—it's helpful. It creates clarity.

The same goes for your strategic planning process. You are not over communicating. In fact, you're giving your people the confidence to move forward.

And that starts with your very first message.

Your First Big Move: The Overview Email

The first formal message you'll send is what we call the **over-view email**. This is your tone-setter. It reconnects everyone to the conversation you started in your board meeting, outlines what's coming, and gives people one clear thing to do next.

Let's pause there: Every email should have a clear call to action.

People are busy, and they want to be helpful—but only if they know what's expected. A great overview email gives them everything they need without making them guess.

———————————

Here's a sample email structure for the Level One - Survey Only Group to get you started:

LEVEL ONE – STAKEHOLDER SURVEY EXAMPLE

Subject Line: Your Voice Matters — Strategic Planning Survey

Hi [Name],

We're kicking off a new strategic planning process for [Organization Name], and we would love your input.

You've been invited to take part in this first step because you know our organization and have valuable perspective to share.

Here are the next steps:

Step 1: Read the Executive Brief (attached). This 1-page summary gives you a quick overview of where the organization stands right now—our mission, current stats, and recent milestones.

Step 2: Complete the short stakeholder survey. Your input will help us better understand what's working, what could be stronger, and what goals matter most moving forward. The survey is anonymous and takes just 5–10 minutes.

Your Action Item: Please complete the survey by [insert due date]. [Insert survey link here]

Thanks again for being part of this process. Your voice helps shape our future.

Warmly,

[Your Name]
[Your Role, if applicable]

Here's a sample email structure for the <u>Core Planning Group</u> to get you started:

LEVEL TWO – STAKEHOLDER SURVEY EXAMPLE

Subject Line: You're Invited to Help Shape Our Strategic Plan

Hi [Name],

You've been invited to be part of our Core Planning Group for Strategic Planning—the small team helping shape the future of [Organization Name]. Your perspective is essential to this process.

This group will meet on [insert date and time] to discuss potential goals, timelines, and co-create the final strategic planning document. Most of the prep work happens ahead of time—so our time together can be focused, collaborative, and productive.

Here's how the strategic planning process works:

Step 1: Read the Executive Brief (attached). This 1-page overview shares where the organization stands today—mission, milestones, key stats, and recent progress.

Step 2: Complete the Stakeholder Survey. This short survey (5–10 minutes) invites your early input. What's working? What could be stronger? What priorities should guide our future?

Step 3: Prioritize the Draft Goals (coming soon). In the coming weeks, you'll receive a short list of proposed goals (based on survey input from all stakeholders). You'll help us sort them by importance before the meeting.

Step 4: Save the Date — Strategic Planning Meeting on [insert date and time]. Please reserve this date on your calendar. It will be our dedicated time to align and finalize our one-page plan.

Your Action Items:
- ☑ Read the Executive Brief
- ☑ Complete the survey by [insert due date] [Insert survey link here]

Thank you for being part of this. Your voice and insight will help us build a plan that guides our organization forward and is ready to put into action.

Warmly,

[Your Name]
[Your Role, if applicable]

What If People Push Back?

If someone raises concerns about the process, don't panic. That's normal. Most people are used to the old way—long meetings, sticky notes, and lots of circling around ideas.

This is different. But not threatening.

Here's how you can respond:

- **Affirm their role:** Let them know they'll have time to talk in person. No decisions are being made before that.
- **Explain the benefit:** The only thing that's changing is how input is gathered—*before* the meeting—so the group has more to work with when you're together.
- **Be transparent:** Everyone will see the same information. Nothing's happening behind closed doors.

Honestly? The biggest skeptics often become your biggest champions. They're unsure at first, but once they experience how grounded and clear the process feels, they're all in.

How to Make Your Emails Actually Work

Let's be real—most people scan emails. Your job is to make them scannable.

Here are a few formatting tricks that make a difference:

- Use **headings** to break things up.
- **Bold** the one sentence or phrase you really want them to see.
- *Italicize* something only if it needs emotional emphasis.

- Use white space generously—don't make it feel like a wall of text.

Think about your email like a signpost, not a novel.

When to Follow Up (and How)

People forget. You'll need to send at least one reminder about the survey.

Here's how to keep it simple and kind:

- **Use BCC** so no one sees who has or hasn't responded.
- Send a reminder on **day 3** and again on **day 5** after the first email only to the people who have not completed the survey.
- Keep it short.

Here's an example reminder text (*if texting is appropriate for your organization***) for the survey:**

> Just a quick reminder to complete the stakeholder survey if you haven't already. It takes 5–10 minutes, and your input is incredibly valuable. Here's the link: [Insert link] Thanks so much for helping us shape our future of [insert organization name]

That's it. Polite, clear, no pressure.

Why This Step Is So Important

This is where your tone gets set. You're telling your team, "This will be different—and in a good way."

When your communication is clear, warm, and steady, people start to trust the process. And when they trust the process, they show up ready.

You don't need to be the world's best writer. You just need to be intentional, honest, and easy to follow.

———————————

Action Steps

- Draft your overview email using the template above or via the email example in the appendix.
- Attach your Executive Brief and include a clear, single call to action.
- Send your first and second reminder emails for 3 and 5 days after.
- Prep yourself to respond with clarity if people are hesitant about the process.

Chapter Review

- Strategic planning communication needs **repetition, clarity, and kindness.**
- Your first email sets the tone for the entire process.
- Resistance is normal—and often temporary.

- A well-formatted email increases the chance people will read and act.
- You don't have to overdo it. You just have to be clear, direct, and thoughtful.

12

ANALYZING SURVEY RESPONSES

You've done it—you sent out your strategic planning survey, and the responses are rolling in. This is where the real insights start to take shape. The voices of your stakeholders are here, in black and white, ready to help shape your next three years.

By reading through the survey data, you're accomplishing three powerful things at once.

Three Steps to Survey Data Analysis

First, you're identifying patterns—what ideas are recurring, where energy is gathering, and what's surfacing as a priority.

Second, you're crafting a high-level summary that brings everyone into the conversation without drowning them in data.

Third, you're building a clear, usable list of stakeholder-generated goals—ready to be prioritized in the next phase.

These three steps turn a stack of open-ended feedback into something organized, actionable, and deeply grounded in real voices.

What to Expect

Don't be surprised if a lot of the responses reflect continuity. Many people will say some version of: "Keep doing what you're doing." That doesn't mean your organization is stagnant—it means your stakeholders see value in the current work and want to protect it.

You might find:

- Practical, actionable suggestions ("improve onboarding," "add a mentorship program")
- Internal priorities ("better communication between board and staff," "update our policies")
- Big dreams ("open a second location," "expand statewide")
- Foundational needs ("stabilize funding," "clarify leadership roles")

You'll also see variety. That's good. Your job isn't to narrow it down yet—it's to absorb what's here.

Read Responses Thoughtfully

Print them out or read them on screen—whatever feels manageable. Grab a highlighter or open a notes doc. Start by reading every single response with an open mind.

Don't try to categorize yet. Just notice. What words keep coming up? What ideas make you nod? What surprises you?

This is where you build your facilitator instincts. You're learning how your group sees the organization—and you're laying the groundwork for a better conversation later.

Some responses might feel critical or even emotional. That's okay. It means people care. Let the hard comments sit with you for a minute—but don't take them personally. You're not here to defend the past. You're here to understand the present.

What to Do with the Executive Brief Feedback

Look at responses to your first question: What's missing from the Executive Brief?

Most people won't have edits. But if someone catches a missing milestone, key moment, or shift in focus—pay attention.

If someone points out a meaningful omission or insight—especially something that was echoed by others—consider adding it to the brief. It shows you're listening.

You're not rewriting the whole thing. You're simply acknowledging any key context you might have missed.

Once you finalize the Executive Brief with any necessary updates, this final version becomes part of your meeting packet—for both you as the facilitator and for the entire core planning group. It's a shared snapshot of your organization's current reality.

That updated brief says: "Here's where we've been. Here's where we are. Now let's decide where to go next."

You want this moment to be a gentle closing of the past, giving you permission to move forward together.

How to Use AI to Clarify Potential Goals

After you've done your personal read-through, AI can help you organize what you're seeing. Think of it as your assistant.

Try prompts like these:

- **To identify recurring goals:***"What distinct goals or ideas are mentioned in these responses? Please group similar ones together and count how many times each is mentioned."*
- **To summarize the overall tone and themes:***"What overall tone and themes show up in these strategic planning survey responses? Please summarize in 3–5 bullet points."*
- **To help prep for the Priority Sort:***"Please create a clean, deduplicated list of goal statements based on these responses. These will be used in a strategic planning priority sort."*

"Deduplicated" just means removing any duplicates from a list—so if the same goal or idea shows up more than once in slightly different ways, you combine or group them together to avoid repeating the same thing.

For example, if five people mention something like:

- "Improve volunteer training"
- "Better training for new volunteers"
- "Training process for volunteer onboarding"

You'd **deduplicate** those into one streamlined idea like: **"Improve volunteer onboarding and training."**

That way, when you create your Priority Sort or share a clean list with your team, you're not showing five versions of the same goal—it's all grouped neatly under one umbrella.

Always double-check what AI gives you. It's a flashlight, not a compass. You're still the guide.

You are the context-holder. AI can surface patterns, but only you know what matters most in your organization's story.

Privacy Reminder: Before using any AI tool, strip out names and identifying info. Use general labels like "Staff Member," "Board Member," or "Parent Volunteer."

Drafting a Summary for the Meeting Packet

Create a one-paragraph summary of what the survey revealed. Think tone over statistics. This summary goes in your board packet or meeting handout. It provides the core planning group insight into the survey data without having to comb through individual responses and spend precious meeting time synthesizing information.

Use this prompt: *"Summarize these strategic planning survey responses in one paragraph. Focus on tone, key themes, and overall direction. Avoid exact counts or metrics—capture the sentiment and shared hopes that emerge across responses."*

Example Response:

"Survey responses showed a strong appreciation for current programs, with a desire to improve internal communication and volunteer retention. Stakeholders emphasized the need to balance

growth with stability, and many expressed hope for deeper community partnerships in the years ahead."

Prepare the Goal List

As you read, you'll naturally start jotting down the different ideas and goals people mention. This isn't about deciding what's important—it's about capturing everything. That full list becomes the raw material for your Priority Sort in the next chapter.

You've taken a big pile of narrative data and turned it into usable insight. That's the heart of facilitation.

Action Steps

- Read every response once through with no agenda
- Highlight repeating ideas or new insights
- Summarize edits (if any) to the Executive Brief
- Use AI to cluster responses and count goal mentions
- Create a one-paragraph summary of survey results to include in your meeting packet
- Build a list of all individual goals mentioned for the Priority Sort

Chapter Review

- Stakeholder input often reflects both stability and aspiration
- Reading for tone and repetition is as important as counting
- Your Executive Brief may need small updates—now is the time
- AI tools help, but your personal read is irreplaceable
- This process transforms raw feedback into focused planning material

13

ALEX'S STORY: FEEDBACK

The survey had been sent. Reminders followed. And now, Alex sat at her desk with a warm mug of mint tea, laptop open, and a thick printout of responses in her lap.

Thirty-seven stakeholders had been invited to share their thoughts—board members, long-time volunteers, teachers, even a few parents from partner schools. Alex had hoped maybe half would respond.

But the final tally made her blink twice: 80%.

She smiled, equal parts astonished and grateful. That kind of turnout wasn't just luck—it was trust. People had taken time out of their week to reflect on BrightStart Readers. And now, it was her job to read every word.

But it hadn't all been smooth.

A few days earlier, Tom—a longtime board member—had replied to her survey email with a pointed concern and had cc'd the board president.

"This doesn't feel like strategic planning to me," he wrote. "I've always believed those decisions need to be made face to face. I'm worried this survey will dilute real conversation—and I don't want to lose my voice in a spreadsheet."

Alex had stared at the message, heart sinking. Tom wasn't just any board member. He had been part of BrightStart for nearly a decade, through lean years and big leaps. His steady presence carried weight. And truthfully? He wasn't wrong to want thoughtful conversation.

But Alex also knew something he didn't: too often, the loudest voices dominated in-person meetings, while quieter ones held back. The survey wasn't replacing discussion—it was opening the door for more people to walk through it.

Still, Tom needed more than a well-written reply.

She asked Shannon, the board president, to join her for a short coffee meeting with him that Friday morning.

The three of them sat at a corner table in the bustling neighborhood café. The smell of espresso and cinnamon lingered in the air. Tom sipped his black coffee, Alex stirred her tea, and Shannon broke off a piece of a shared scone.

Tom explained his concern—not just about the format, but about being sidelined. "I've seen a lot of processes where people collect input just to check a box," he said. "Then the real decisions get made in a room I'm not in."

Alex nodded. "We'll still meet—in person, as a group. That meeting matters and it's where the plan will be formed with consensus from the group. And this data collection ahead of time helps us show up better prepared. This survey isn't replacing the work—it's preparing us for it."

Tom looked unconvinced, arms remained folded. But then he sighed. "Okay. I'll go along with it. But I'm still a little skeptical."

Alex offered a grateful smile. "Totally fair. Let's just try it and see."

It wasn't a full endorsement—but it was enough.

Back at her office, reading through the responses, she felt a new kind of nervous energy.

The first thing she noticed? Most people didn't want dramatic change. They expressed appreciation for BrightStart's current work. One wrote,

---

"Please don't fix what isn't broken—we're making a difference."

Another said simply,

"Keep doing what you're doing. Just more of it."

Alex's shoulders dropped a little. One of her own ideas—expanding to middle-grade tutoring—hadn't been mentioned. Not even once. But still, she kept reading.

She highlighted phrases that stood out:

"Can we offer virtual mentoring for kids in remote areas?"

"More training for volunteers would help with consistency."

"We should partner with the library for family reading nights."

And then there were the vision responses.

Alex's favorite question had been:

What would it look like if BrightStart was wildly successful in three years?

The answers there *sparked*.

One parent wrote:

"I see a program in every elementary school in our region— volunteers greeting kids by name, books in every backpack."

Another said:

"We're known as the go-to reading support for young learners. Teachers request us. Families celebrate us."

One especially bold response suggested BrightStart establish an *annual community reading festival*, complete with author visits, book giveaways, and student storytellers.

Alex underlined that one twice.

She spent a full evening reading, then a second day with her highlighter. She made margin notes, typed up thoughts, and even whispered a few "Yes!" moments to herself.

One data point a respondent mentioned—tracking volunteer retention year over year—wasn't something she had included in the original brief. But it was a great addition. Volunteer consistency directly impacted student support.

She updated the Executive Brief to reflect the new metric, ran it past Shannon, and added the revised version to her meeting packet.

Then she opened ChatGPT and asked:

- *"List all the distinct goals mentioned in these responses. Group similar ones."*
- *"What themes or tone show up across these answers?"*

The AI generated a list: 27 distinct goal ideas, grouped into five rough categories. It was helpful—but Alex still read through each one again to make sure nothing had been misread or flattened.

Then came the next step: drafting a clean summary of the survey results. A few lines that would capture the heartbeat of what she'd read. She typed:

> *"Stakeholders expressed deep appreciation for the program's current structure, with a strong desire to maintain quality while scaling responsibly. Many called for improved volunteer training and communication between board and staff. The vision responses revealed hope for broader community presence, more school partnerships, and new events that celebrate literacy in joyful, visible ways."*

She placed that just after the brief in the draft meeting packet for the strategic planning in-person meeting.

Finally, she turned to the biggest job yet: building the full goal list.

She read through her AI summary again, her own notes, and frowned. Twenty-seven goals felt... heavy.

How would she present these in a way that felt focused—not overwhelming? Should she group them by theme? Rank them by how often they were mentioned? Would she risk oversimplifying?

Her screen still glowed in front of her. A blinking cursor waited at the top of a blank document: **Priority Sort: Draft List of Goals.**

She reached for her papers——and paused.

The work could wait until morning.

Tonight, her daughter had a school concert. The laundry still sat in the dryer. And if she was honest, her brain needed to cool off.

But even as she packed up her things and shut down her laptop, one thought followed her out the door:

The way I shape this next step matters.

This was the moment it hit her: her role as facilitator carried a new kind of responsibility.

The way she interpreted these survey responses—the way she grouped goals, removed duplicates, and gave each one a name—would shape how the core planning group saw the priorities. If she oversimplified, a valuable nuance might be lost. If she was too detailed, the group might lose the thread. This was the bridge between insight and action.

Tomorrow, she'd sit down with fresh eyes. She'd take all those goals—dozens of them—and turn them into something clear, honest, and ready to be sorted.

But for now, she slipped on her coat, grabbed her keys, and let the next step wait.

Because being a good facilitator?It wasn't about rushing forward.

It was about showing up steady.

And tomorrow, she'd be ready.

Because what came next might be the most delicate step of all.

And she wasn't sure how to begin.

14

CREATING A PRIORITY SORT

I magine this: In a traditional model, you've sent out a stakeholder survey and you're about to walk into the planning meeting. Everyone brings their opinions, and you're expected to guide the conversation. But you have no idea which ideas are most important to the group. The conversation veers off track. Voices compete. Time runs out.

Now picture something different: You walk into that same room already knowing where the group agrees—and where they don't. You know which goals are must-haves, which ones need discussion, and which don't have traction at all. That's the power of the priority sort.

This one step can completely transform your planning session from chaotic to clear. It reveals the patterns in stakeholder input and gives you a shared map to navigate by.

The idea was first introduced to me in a completely different context—a card sort from a tech company looking for user input on future product features. I was handed cards labeled with different software components and asked to organize them by priority. It was simple, but powerful. And it stuck with me.

Over time, I adapted that process to strategic planning. Now, it's one of the most powerful tools in the Clarity Method— and one that surprises most people. Because they've never seen this kind of alignment data visualized before. But once they do? It unlocks the conversation. It brings a sense of calm. It makes people feel proud of what they already agree on— and more open to discussing where they don't.

Let's walk through how to build it.

Try It Yourself: A Low-Stakes Priority Sort

Before we dive into the structure for your organization, try this quick, playful version of a priority sort. It helps you step into the mindset of sorting and rating ideas.

Imagine you and a group of friends are planning a weekend getaway.

Here are your options:

- Beach weekend
- Cabin in the mountains
- City food tour
- National park hiking trip
- Amusement park adventure

Each person ranks these choices in one of four categories: High Priority, Medium Priority, Low Priority, and Not Important.

Then, you compile the results which typically look like a table into a visual grid—a heat map—that shows how many people rated each option in each category.

Here's what that might look like:

Priority Sort Results
(Sample Heat Map with Textures)

FRIEND RATINGS

	HIGH	MEDIUM	LOW	NOT IMP.
BEACH	6	1	0	0
CABIN	0	1	4	3
CITY	1	5	1	0
PARK	2	2	2	1
AMUSEMENT	0	0	6	1

WEEKEND GETAWAY

Reading the map is more powerful than looking at a simple table. The shades and textures show how many people placed each trip option in each category. Even without color, the patterns stand out:

- **Beach weekend** has the most High Priority ratings—it's a strong favorite.
- **City food tour** drew the most Medium scores—people are open to it.
- **Amusement park adventure** leans heavily toward Low Priority—not a crowd favorite.

The heat map provides a visual representation of agreement and disagreement in a fast, easy-to-understand graphic that should be included in your strategic meeting agenda packet.

————————————

From Ideas to Priorities

By now, you've reviewed the survey responses, grouped similar ideas, and distilled them into a list of 10 to 30 potential goals. These aren't polished statements yet—just the raw materials that came from your people.

This is where the next layer of clarity begins.

The priority sort is a second, short survey where you ask your stakeholders to rank each potential goal by how important they believe it is.

No brainstorming. No back-and-forth debate. Just focused input—gathered before the meeting.

How Priority Sorting Works

Let's say one of your survey responses suggested "launching a community reading festival."

That idea becomes a goal on your priority sort.

Each person you send it to will categorize that idea (and every other one) as:

- High Priority
- Medium Priority
- Low Priority
- Not Relevant / Not Important Right Now

That's it. Simple categories that give you a heat map of how the group feels.

You'll quickly see which ideas have strong support—and which don't.

This saves *so much* meeting time. Instead of spending hours figuring out what matters, you'll walk in already knowing.

Why This Step Works

Let's be honest—meetings can get messy. The group spends half the time deciding what to talk about...and not enough time actually deciding.

The priority sort changes that.

It reveals:

- Where your team is aligned
- Where you need to have real conversation
- Which goals are non-starters

It also makes your planning meeting smoother, faster, and

more focused. You'll spend less time guessing and more time prioritizing.

And here's the key insight: For the first time in the process, you now have some *knowns*.

You will likely see goals that have strong consensus—and others that are clearly not supported. This allows you and your planning group to begin a pencil sketch of which goals might belong on the final plan. Instead of feeling like you're starting with a big, overwhelming blank slate, the group gets to begin with clarity. That sigh of relief? It's real. You're narrowing the field. You're focusing in. And that's when real progress begins.

How to Set It Up

Take your survey response themes and turn them into clear, distinct goals. Even if several people mentioned the same thing, it only needs to appear once.

Guidelines to keep in mind:

- **Stick to under 30 goals.** If you have more, combine similar ones carefully.
- **Don't add a write-in option.** This isn't the time for new ideas—just sorting.
- **Be clear.** Use everyday language your team understands.
- **Use simple tools.** Google Forms, SurveyMonkey, or Typeform all work well.

- **Utilize the Ranking Question form**. Every survey tool will have a version of forced rank choice question which you can use to create your priority sort.
- **Require sorting on each goal.** Make each potential goal required for sorting.
- **Give a deadline.** 3–5 business days is ideal. Follow up if needed.
- **Explain the purpose.** This isn't about making decisions yet—it's about seeing the landscape.

How to Create a Priority Sort Google Form (Sample Setup)

Form Title:

Strategic Planning Priority Sort

Form Description:

Thank you for taking the time to complete this short priority sort. These goals were pulled directly from the first round of stakeholder feedback. Your input will help us understand where the team is aligned and where more discussion is needed.

Please rate each of the following goals based on how important you believe they are for our organization's success over the next three years. This survey is anonymous and should take no more than 10–15 minutes.

For Each Goal, Use a Multiple Choice Grid or Linear Scale Question

But the best layout for your goals is a **Multiple Choice Grid**, with your goals as rows and these 4 options as columns:

Question Title:

Please rate the following potential goals using the scale below:

Sample Rows [insert your own goals pulled from survey results here]:

Ex. Launch a community mentoring program for youth

Ex. Expand fundraising efforts through new grant partnerships

Ex. Improve volunteer training and onboarding

Columns:

High Priority

Medium Priority

Low Priority

Not Important at this Time

Settings Tip:

1. Toggle "Require a response in each row" to **ON**
2. Keep the form anonymous by not collecting emails unless needed

3. Add a short description below the grid if desired:
   "There are no right or wrong answers. Just sort based on your honest sense of what will have the biggest impact."

Wrap-Up Message

Confirmation Message: Thank you for sharing your input! These results will help shape the discussion in our upcoming strategic planning session. Your voice makes a difference.

A Note on Grouping Goals

It's okay to combine similar ideas—but do it with care. If one person said "open a thrift shop" and another said "start a gift shop," you might group them into: *"Open a retail fundraising shop."*

But don't combine goals that aren't truly the same.

Remember: people will be scanning for *their* ideas.

If they don't see something they said reflected, it can feel like their voice was skipped. That's a trust-breaker. Be generous and transparent in how you represent the input.

The Switzerland Principle

As facilitator, you are *Switzerland* here.

You are neutral. Your job is not to decide which goals are valid or important.

If a unique idea came up—even if only once—it deserves a

place in the sort. Your role is to reflect what was said, not to shape it.

Later, the group will decide what actually gets into the plan. But this step is about surfacing all possibilities.

What If Priorities Conflict?

That's actually a good sign.

You might have one goal about expanding services, and another about tightening focus. Include both.

When people have to rate each one individually, you'll start to see where tensions lie—and where alignment begins.

Better to discover this now than to be blindsided in the room.

How to Communicate the Priority Sort

Just like with your first survey, your communication matters:

- Keep the tone respectful, clear, and brief.
- Share the link with a quick summary of why this matters.
- Thank people for their time—and remind them that their input shaped this list.
- Give a clear due date.
- Follow up using BCC, just like before.

Here's a sample email template to send your core planning group:

PRIORITY SORT SURVEY EXAMPLE

Subject Line: Strategic Planning – Help Us Sort Our Priorities

Hi [Name],

Thank you for being part of our strategic planning process. Based on the first round of survey responses, we've compiled a list of potential goals that reflect what our stakeholders value most.

This next step is a short "priority sort." It's anonymous, takes about 10–15 minutes, and helps us understand where the group is aligned—and where more discussion may be needed.

What to Do:

1. Click the link. [insert link to priority sort survey]

2. Rate each goal as High, Medium, Low, or Not Important.

You don't need to justify your choices—just sort them thoughtfully. Your responses won't lock you in or make decisions for the group. They give us a starting point for the in-person meeting.

Priority Sort Link: [Insert link here]
Due Date: [Insert due date here]

Thank you for your voice in this process. This sort is based entirely on what you and others shared in the first survey. We're simply taking the next step—together.

With appreciation,

[Your Name]
[Your Role, if applicable]

What This Step Accomplishes

This process transforms your strategic planning meeting.

Instead of walking in with a list of ideas and trying to get through them all... you'll walk in with:

- A full map of where people agree and where they don't
- A short list of top contenders
- Clarity on what still needs discussion
- Confidence in how the group will move forward

You're giving the group a head start.

They're not starting from zero—they're starting from insight.

———————————

Action Steps

- Turn your survey responses into 10–30 clear, distinct goals
- Build a short priority sort using Google Forms or another survey tool
- Invite all core planning group members to complete it within 3–5 days
- Follow up to ensure responses
- Prepare to analyze the results for trends and alignment

Chapter Review

The priority sort is a fast, inclusive way to understand your team's priorities

- It surfaces alignment *and* tension before your meeting
- Facilitators must remain neutral—every idea deserves representation

- This step turns a messy meeting into a focused, efficient planning session

15

MAKING SENSE OF THE DATA

Take a second to remember where you started: back at the moment when strategic planning facilitation was handed to you. It felt undefined. Like anything—and everything—was on the table. You didn't yet know what success looked like, what conversations you'd need to guide, or even where to begin.

But now? Now you've built your executive brief, created stakeholder surveys, and facilitated a priority sort that gave your planning group the chance to weigh in—quietly, thoughtfully, and anonymously. And that brings us here.

This is the turning point in the process.

You're about to uncover what matters most to your team— not based on hunches or loud voices, but through real, tangible data. This is where patterns start to emerge, tensions come to the surface, and—for the first time—a sketch of your future plan starts to take shape.

Let's get into it.

What This Tells You About Your Meeting

The priority sort results are more than numbers on a chart—they're insight into how your team thinks. With this data in hand, you're walking into your meeting with:

- **Strong agreement?** You'll spend your meeting time on plan-building, not debating.
- **High disagreement?** You'll need structured time to talk through tensions and reach clarity.
- **Mostly neutrality?** Your team might need more context—or they're waiting for leadership direction.

Either way, you now have knowns.

And knowns = momentum.

Getting Your Data Ready

Start by exporting your priority sort responses (from Google Forms, Typeform, or your platform of choice) into a spreadsheet. Each row should represent one stakeholder. Each column represents a goal. And each cell holds their ranking—High, Medium, Low, or Not Important.

It won't make sense at first glance. That's normal. Think of it like a puzzle—jumbled pieces at first, but the image gets clearer the longer you look.

What You're Gaining

This is the first time in the process that you're working with *knowns*. You'll see which goals have strong consensus—and which don't. That gives you (and your group) a sigh of relief. Instead of feeling like everything's wide open, you now have some clarity. The unknown becomes manageable.

That's your edge as a facilitator.

It also gives you something else: your first sketch of a plan. You'll start to see which goals are likely headed for the final draft—and which might not make the cut.

Why Use AI Here?

Analyzing priority sort data by hand is doable—but time consuming. AI tools like ChatGPT or Claude can help you speed up the process without sacrificing insight. It's like having a trusted assistant who can sort, summarize, and surface patterns—while you stay focused on the human side of facilitation.

Want a heat map? AI can give you the structure and even generate a formatted version. Want to know where agreement is strongest? AI can show you the numbers behind the patterns.

Just remember: AI is your assistant—not your decider.

You're still the one making the meaning.

What to Prompt (and Why)

Prompt 1: Analyze Frequency of Responses

"I have a spreadsheet of survey responses from stakeholders who ranked each strategic goal using these categories: High Priority, Medium Priority, Low Priority, Not Important. Each row represents one stakeholder's response. Each column represents a different goal.

Please help me analyze this data by:

- *Highlighting goals with the highest agreement (e.g. mostly High or mostly Not Important)*
- *Identifying goals with neutrality*
- *Identifying goals with the most disagreement"*

Why: This gives you the big picture. You'll quickly see which goals are rising to the top and where your group is split.

What to do with it: Use this insight to build your "Consensus Goals" and "Discussion Goals" lists. These will go in your meeting packet.

Prompt 2: Create a Heat Map Structure

"Based on this priority sort data, can you help me create a table or heat map that shows the distribution of responses for each goal across the four categories: High, Medium, Low, Not Important? Please use textures or grayscale labels instead of color."

Why: Heat maps make it visual. And when you're in the meeting, being able to *show* agreement or tension makes your job easier.

What to do with it: Include this heat map in your facilitator packet—and consider including it in the core planning group's meeting materials too.

Prompt 3: Draft a Summary for the Meeting Packet

"Can you write a one-paragraph summary of the priority sort results in a warm, plain-English tone suitable for a nonprofit board packet?"

Why: This keeps everyone in the loop without overwhelming them with spreadsheets.

What to do with it: Add this paragraph summary to the meeting packet for the full planning group. It helps people feel informed and seen.

What You'll Discover

When you analyze your sort data, you'll start to see three categories emerge:

Areas of Agreement

These are your "green lights." Everyone (or nearly everyone) marked these as High Priority—or everyone agreed they're not needed. These goals can likely move right into the plan or be set aside without debate.

Areas of Neutrality

These are the "maybes." Most people ranked them Medium Priority. They're not controversial, but they're not burning needs either. These might be good for Year Two or Three of your plan.

Areas of Disagreement

These are your hotspots. Some folks marked these goals High Priority, others put them at the bottom. This is where meaningful conversation is needed. These will become your meeting's focus areas.

Analyze a Sample Priority Sort Heat Map with Textures

Priority Sort Results
(Sample Heat Map with Textures)

CORE PLANNING GROUP RATINGS

	HIGH	MEDIUM	LOW	NOT IMP.
IDEA A	6	1	0	0
IDEA B	0	1	3	3
IDEA C	1	4	1	0
IDEA D	4	2	1	0
IDEA E	3	2	1	1

GOALS

How to Read This Heat Map:

- **Idea A**: Strong agreement. 6 out of 7 rated it as High Priority, with just 1 rating it Medium. This goal is a likely "must-include."
- **Idea B**: High disagreement. 3 stakeholders marked it Low, 3 said Not Important, and only 1 chose Medium. This goal is almost entirely unsupported—with one outlier.
- **Idea C**: Neutral leaning. Most rated it Medium Priority. This suggests stakeholders aren't strongly

opposed or passionate—might be a "maybe" for Year 2 or 3.

- **Idea D**: Skewed toward High. More than half chose High, with a few Medium or Low—likely worth including but open to further discussion.
- **Idea E**: Mixed. A slight tilt toward importance (3 High, 2 Medium), but with some low or no support.

Action Steps

- Export your sort data to a spreadsheet
- Use AI to summarize and find patterns
- Identify 3 types of goals: agreement, neutrality, disagreement
- Create a visual summary (heat map or chart)
- Add a summary paragraph to the group meeting packet

Chapter Review

- Why AI can be a useful co-pilot in the analysis phase
- Which prompts help you uncover patterns and prepare materials
- How to identify and categorize stakeholder priorities

16

ALEX'S STORY: PRIORITIZING

The building was quiet—the kind of quiet that only existed before 8 a.m. Alex had arrived early on purpose. She needed a stretch of time without meetings, emails, or hallway check-ins. Just her, a clear mind, and the next big step in the planning process.

She took a sip of her coffee—extra strong, half-sweet, from her favorite neighborhood café—and opened her laptop.

The document in front of her was titled:

Priority Sort – Draft Goal List.

Twenty-seven goals. Each one pulled directly from the stakeholder survey. No editing for preference. No cutting based on how many people mentioned it. Just clean phrasing, grouped by theme, and stripped of jargon.

Some were immediately familiar:

- Improve volunteer onboarding
- Strengthen school partnerships
- Host family reading nights

Others pushed the boundaries a little more:

- Launch a regional reading festival
- Create a leadership development track for mentors

She scrolled slowly, double-checking for clarity. The wording mattered. If people didn't see their idea reflected—or didn't understand what the goal meant—it could erode trust in the process.

Then she opened Google Forms and began to build.

Each goal went into a multiple-choice grid. The rating options were simple:

- **High Priority**
- **Medium Priority**
- **Low Priority**
- **Not Important at This Time**

But before the list began, she added this note:

"This isn't a final vote—just a way to help us get organized. These goals came directly from the ideas shared in our first survey, and now we're asking for your help to get a sense of where there's alignment and where we might need more discussion.

Your responses will help us walk into the upcoming planning meeting with a clearer picture—not to make decisions ahead of time, but to make that meeting smoother and more focused.

We'll talk through everything together in person. That's where the real decisions happen—what goes in the plan, what the timeline looks like, and how we move forward as a team."

She paused. Reread. It struck the right tone: respectful, clear, and grounded in collaboration.

Then she drafted the email to send the form to her core planning group.

She read it once more, then hit send.

Done.

Well—almost done.

As the responses rolled in over the next few days, she watched the spreadsheet fill with quiet decisions. Each cell told a story of preference, hope, disagreement, alignment.

And when the final few responses came in, she turned to her digital assistant for help:

"Help me analyze this priority sort data. Which goals have the strongest agreement? Which are neutral? And which are most divided?"

The patterns emerged quickly.

Some goals had near-universal support. Others were clearly divisive. A few hovered in the land of "maybe"—not dismissed, not celebrated.

Then she created the heat map.

Even in grayscale, the trends jumped off the page.

- Clear consensus.
- Mixed reactions.
- Disagreements that would need real airtime.

It was all there.

Alex printed the heat map and set it aside.

She leaned back in her chair, the heat map still glowing on the screen.

At first, she'd just planned to email the results and bring a printed agenda to the meeting. But now? Now she could feel the shift.

This wasn't just another board conversation. It was shaping up to be the biggest meeting she'd ever led.

Thirteen people would be in the room. Some had decades of history with BrightStart. Others were new but already invested. Everyone had an opinion—and everyone would be looking to her to guide the discussion.

That realization brought a flutter of nerves.

She opened her desk drawer and pulled out a clean white binder. Something about holding paper—real paper—made her feel steadier. Grounded.

She started printing.

The full set of survey responses—just in case someone wanted to trace a goal back to a comment. The summary paragraph she'd written to capture the heart of what people had said. The complete list of raw goal ideas. The cleaned-up, condensed version that went into the sort. The priority sort data, heat map included. And the short narrative she'd written to explain what the heat map actually showed.

She slid each page into its own sleeve and clipped them into place.

Why the binder?

Because when she stood at the front of that meeting room, her laptop would be connected to the projector—displaying the working version of the plan as they shaped it live. She wouldn't have time to hunt through files or search her inbox.

If someone had a question—about the wording of a goal, or where it came from—she wanted to be able to flip to the answer in seconds. Not because she needed to be the expert, but because she needed to be steady.

This binder wasn't about control.

It was about care.

It reminded her: *you've done the work.* You're not walking into that room alone. You're walking in prepared—with the voices of the team behind you, and the structure to hold the space.

She placed the binder in her tote bag and jotted one more note on the yellow pad beside her:

Meeting Flow: How will I guide them through this?

Because the next step wasn't just about sharing the data.

It was about *how* she would help the group make sense of it—together.

And the real work of facilitation was about to begin.

17

PREPARING EFFECTIVE MEETING PACKETS

The night before the meeting, you might find yourself lying awake, running through mental checklists.

Did I print enough copies? What if someone challenges the timeline? What if the conversation goes off track—or stalls out completely?

You're not just leading a meeting. You're facilitating decisions that will shape the next few years of your organization's work. That's a big moment.

But here's the thing—how you prepare now will shape how you show up in that room.

And nothing will give you more peace of mind—or practical power—than a well-built meeting packet.

This is your facilitator's safety net. Your compass. Your confidence boost when the conversation gets complicated.

When you have the right materials in your hands—clearly

organized, thoughtful, and complete—you can walk into the room knowing:

- You're ready for the curveballs.
- You're grounded in the data.
- You're not carrying the whole thing in your head.

And your stakeholders? They feel that steadiness, too.

A clear, clean packet helps them engage without feeling over-whelmed. It sets the tone: *We've done the work. Let's focus and build together.*

This chapter will walk you through exactly how to prepare two versions of your meeting materials:

1. A **Facilitator Packet** that equips you to lead with confidence
2. A **Stakeholder Packet** that keeps your team aligned and engaged

Think of it like this: you're building two maps. One detailed and marked-up—for the guide (that's you). And one simpli-fied, easy to follow—for the hikers walking beside you.

Let's get you ready to lead.

——————————

Your Facilitator Packet: Be Over-prepared

Your packet should be thorough. Exceptionally thorough. This is the version you'll want to organize in a three-ring binder with tabs so you can find exactly what you need, exactly when you need it.

Strategic planning conversations are living, breathing things. People ask questions you don't expect. Emotions can flare. Perspectives shift in real time.

Having the right document at your fingertips can save the moment—and refocus the room.

———————————

What to Include in Your Facilitator Packet

Here's what I recommend, divided into five tabs:

Tab 1: Meeting Agenda and Overview

- The detailed agenda with time blocks (we will craft the agenda in the next chapter)

Tab 2: Executive Brief

- The one-page summary that closes out the previous planning cycle
- Any background notes or context your group might need

Tab 3: Raw Survey Data

- Complete printouts of all stakeholder responses
- Your handwritten notes, themes, or standout observations

- Any AI-generated summaries you've used

Tab 4: Priority Sort Analysis

- Raw priority sort responses
- A heat map or chart showing patterns
- A summary of consensus goals vs. discussion goals
- Any AI-generated summaries you've used

Tab 5: Draft Strategic Plan

- Your early ideas (in pencil!) of how goals could sequence across 1–3 years
- Notes about goal dependencies or things that need to happen first in the timeline
- Blank planning templates to fill out with the group in real time

You most likely won't use everything in this binder—but having it ready gives you presence, confidence, and backup when you need it most.

———————

The Stakeholder Packet: Clear, Clean, and Focused

Your planning team doesn't need all the raw data or detailed notes. Their packet should be easy to scan and easy to use during the meeting—even if they haven't looked at it ahead of time

Page 1: Meeting Agenda

A clear, one-page agenda showing how the meeting will flow.

Page 2: Executive Brief

The agreed-upon summary of where the organization stands now.

Page 3: Survey Summary

Either a one-page summary of themes (preferably) or the complete list of anonymous survey responses. Choose the format that best supports your group's working style.

Page 4: Priority Sort Results

Your heat map or visual summary of stakeholder priorities. Include a short explanation and a simple legend.

Page 5: Blank Planning Template

A blank grid with years across the top and room to record goal ideas. This helps people follow along as you build the plan live during the meeting.

Making the Heat Map Accessible

Most people in the room will never have seen a heat map before, so your job is to translate it in plain language.

Keep it simple on the heat map page in the packet:

- Use colors or icons with a clear key
- Add a short explanation right on the page

Practical Prep Tips

- **Email packets in advance**—but prepare as if they have not studied the packet

- **Bring printed copies** to the meeting.
- **Tab your facilitator binder** for quick access.
- **Keep raw data nearby** but don't hand it out unless someone asks.
- **Include a notes grid** in every stakeholder packet to support real-time engagement.

Why This Level of Preparation Pays Off

Facilitation isn't about being the smartest person in the room. It's about creating the conditions for other smart people to work well together.

When your participants feel prepared, they're more thoughtful and more present.When *you* feel prepared, you can focus on listening and leading—not scrambling for files or guessing at what comes next.

This is how you take a group from "we don't even know where to start" to "look what we built—together."

You're not winging it.

You're walking in ready.

Action Steps

- **Build your facilitator packet** using a three-ring binder and clearly labeled tabs. Include all data, notes, and potential planning tools.
- **Create a streamlined stakeholder packet** that's simple, skimmable, and designed for real-time participation.
- **Print everything** and bring extra copies. Assume people won't read in advance, but will follow along in the room if materials are clear and engaging.

Chapter Review

- Your facilitator packet is more than just a backup—it's a confidence tool that lets you stay calm and responsive in real time.
- A clear stakeholder packet helps your planning group show up prepared, reduces confusion, and keeps the conversation productive.
- You don't have to have every answer—but when you're organized, you can guide the group with clarity and composure.
- Preparing your materials ahead of time means you can focus on people and process—not printing and scrambling.
- The way you prepare shapes the way others participate. Thoughtful packets signal that this work matters—and that their voices do, too.

18

DESIGNING THE MEETING AGENDA

This is the meeting where it all comes together.

You've done the heavy lifting—gathering insight, sorting goals, identifying patterns. But now you're stepping into a new role: guide.

And that means designing an agenda that doesn't just walk through topics—it brings your group into a shared rhythm.

The structure of your meeting matters. Not because you need every minute scheduled, but because the right flow will help people feel grounded, respected, and clear on what comes next.

Let's pause here, because this part is important:

You don't need a rigid script. What you need is a light framework that offers just enough structure at the start—and space to move once conversation begins.

———————

Think of your meeting in three phases:

Phase One: Grounding and Orientation (Approx. 30 minutes)

The beginning of your meeting sets the tone for everything that follows. Your goal in this first phase is to help people feel confident that real progress has already been made—and to invite them into the next step.

This is not a brainstorming session. It's not a blank slate. The work has already begun. Your job is to show them how.

Start with a Warm Welcome and a Process Recap (5 minutes)

Offer a genuine welcome and give a quick overview of what's brought you to this point. You might say:

———————

"Thanks for being here. Over the past month, we've collected feedback, reviewed the data together, and sorted priorities. Today is about building the next chapter of our organization—together."

———————

Briefly review the phases of the planning process so far:

- Stakeholder surveys
- Priority sort
- Summary and analysis
- Packets in front of them today

Walk Through the Meeting Packet (3–5 minutes)

Guide people through the materials in their hands. Call attention to:

- The survey summary
- The priority sort results or heat map
- The blank three-year planning grid

Celebrate the Foundation (7–10 minutes)

Before diving into goals or decisions, ground the group in what's working. Use the Executive Brief to name 2–3 recent wins. Then, briefly revisit the mission and vision.

Introduce the Priority Analysis (10–15 minutes)

Now you'll share the results of your priority sort—typically in the form of a heat map or grouped list. Project the visual and keep the explanation simple:

"This heat map shows where we're aligned and where we're split. Green means strong agreement, yellow means mixed responses, red means we'll need some thoughtful discussion."

Start with the green zones. Then move toward the areas of disagreement. Let the group see the contrast: alignment is real, and differences are manageable.

Phase Two: Collaborative Sorting and Discussion (Approx. 45–60 minutes)

This is where the real facilitation begins. Your job here is to help the group work through each of the proposed goals and decide what belongs in the plan—and when.

Start with the goals where there's strong agreement. Once the high-consensus goals are acknowledged and placed, move to the goals that showed disagreement or ambivalence.

Use your agenda to name them ahead of time. If there are many, group them by theme:

- **Governance:** These are goals related to how the organization is led and managed. Examples might include board development, succession planning, or revisiting bylaws.
- **Programming:** These are the services and activities you deliver to fulfill your mission—tutoring sessions, classes, events, or anything involving direct community impact.
- **Fundraising:** These goals focus on generating income —whether through grants, individual giving, sponsorships, or earned revenue strategies.
- **Community Partnerships:** These include collaborations with schools, libraries, or local businesses that support or extend your work.

For each goal, guide the group in deciding whether it should be:

- High priority (include in the plan now)
- Medium priority (possibly for a later year)
- Low priority (not for this cycle)
- Not relevant (set aside entirely)

Ask questions like:

"What would it take to make this goal realistic?"

"Is this a now goal, or a next-year goal?"

"Are there other goals that are dependent on this goal?"

"How does this align with our mission?"

Phase Three: Building the Plan in Real Time (Approx. 45–60 minutes)

Once the group has sorted and discussed, shift into building mode. Project your blank three-year grid. Start adding the agreed-upon goals in real time.

Start with the easy wins. Then fill in the middle, working together to find a natural, balanced sequence.

Ask questions like:

"What groundwork needs to happen first?"

"Can we realistically do all of this in Year One?"

"How can we stagger our work across three years?"

"Who's the best fit to lead each piece?"

Assigning Preliminary Leads (15–20 minutes)

Once the plan is mapped out, assign preliminary responsibility for each goal. You're not assigning task lists—just identifying point people.

Closing the Meeting (5–10 minutes)

End with clarity and encouragement. Remind everyone:

- What happens next
- When action planning begins
- How progress will be tracked

Sample Agendas: Two Formats to Fit Your Group

Strategic planning doesn't have to take all day. In fact, with the right preparation, this process can be completed in just a few hours. The key is in how you structure the conversation. Below are two sample formats that have worked well for groups of different sizes and complexity.

Comprehensive Agenda (3.5 hours) Ideal for larger groups, complex priorities, or when multiple areas of disagreement need to be worked through.

Focused Agenda (2 hours) Great for smaller teams, tighter alignment, or when you've already worked through most issues beforehand. Yes—it really can be done in this timeframe.

Choosing Your Timeline and Preparing to Share

Now that you've seen both sample agendas, it's time to choose which one is the best fit for your group. I recommend selecting a timeframe in collaboration with the Executive Director or board president. They may have a better sense of scheduling realities, board energy, or any external time constraints.

If you choose the two-hour version and realize during the meeting that more time is needed, it's okay to extend the session by 30–60 minutes or schedule a short follow-up meeting to finalize the plan. But trust me—most groups can complete this process in under three hours when the packets are clear and the facilitation stays on track.

Once the agenda is finalized:

- Print a copy to place at the top of every meeting packet.
- Email the full packet to the core planning group a few days before the meeting.
- In the email, include the agenda, meeting time and location, and a reminder that the meeting will build directly from the stakeholder input they helped provide.

This extra step of early communication helps your group show up prepared, centered, and ready to engage.

Sample Email to Send With Your Meeting Packet

STRATEGIC PLANNING
MEETING PACKET EMAIL

Subject: Strategic Planning Meeting Materials – Please Review Before [Insert Date]

Hi team,

Thank you again for your thoughtful input throughout this strategic planning process. We're getting ready for our in-person planning meeting, and I wanted to share the full meeting packet with you in advance.

Attached, you'll find:

• The **agenda** for our meeting

• A one-page **executive brief** summarizing where we are

• **Survey results** and summary

• Our **priority heat map** analysis

• A **blank planning grid** you can use to follow along or take notes

Meeting Details:

Date: [Insert date]
Time: [Insert time]
Location: [Insert location or Zoom link]

This meeting will build directly from the input you've already shared through the survey and goal ranking. We'll walk through areas of agreement, discuss key priorities, and map out a draft three-year strategic plan—together.

If you have any questions before we meet, feel free to reach out. I'm looking forward to working through this next step with all of you!

Warmly,

[Your name]

You've already done the hard work of preparation. You are informed, equipped, and ready to walk into that room and facilitate a focused, collaborative conversation. Be proud of how far you've brought this process—and trust that you're ready for the next step.

Action Steps

- Draft a flexible meeting agenda with three key phases
- Start with celebration and orientation
- Use your heat map to structure discussion
- Facilitate real-time placement of goals into a plan
- Assign point people to keep the plan moving

Chapter Review

- Strategic planning meetings work best with just enough structure
- Leading with alignment builds momentum and trust
- Collaborative sorting turns tension into clarity
- Real-time building leads to ownership and shared commitment
- Great facilitation isn't about control—it's about clarity and care

19

YOUR DRAFT PLAN: THINKING AHEAD

B efore you step into your strategic planning meeting, you have one more tool to add to your kit: your pencil sketch.

This isn't something you'll project or share. It's for your eyes only—a quiet but powerful behind-the-scenes move that will pay off in clarity and confidence.

Think of it like the visualization techniques Olympians use before competition. They close their eyes and mentally walk through the routine, the run, or the race—so when it's go time, their mind and body already know the rhythm. You're doing the same here, but with goals, timelines, and logic.

You're not planning the plan. You're simply rehearsing how different pieces might fit together—so you're not surprised when the conversation gets tricky or goals overlap in unexpected ways. This mental walk-through sharpens your instincts as a facilitator.

This is your chance to:

- See how the pieces fit
- Catch logical gaps before they happen
- Anticipate where discussion might get stuck or energized

It's a thinking tool. And it's one of the most underrated steps in facilitation.

––––––––––––––

Your Draft Strategic Plan (a.k.a. the Pencil Sketch)

Grab a copy of the three-year planning grid and start sketching.

Ask yourself:

- Which goals are foundational and need to come first?
- Which goals build on others?
- Where are the natural groupings or dependencies?
- How can we balance the workload year by year?

Aim for **no more than three major goals per year**. Fewer is fine. More tends to overload the system and cause burnout.

As you go, you'll start to notice patterns. Maybe several ideas all rely on a shared resource. Maybe one goal unlocks progress for two others. That's the kind of insight you want before you're standing in front of a group.

This draft is not about being right—and it's definitely not about controlling the outcome. It's simply your chance to walk through the logic puzzle in advance. As you sketch, you're not deciding what *should* go in the plan—you're preparing to support your group as they figure it out together.

This quiet exercise helps you anticipate potential sticking points. It reveals where conversations may need more time, where a certain goal might trigger questions, or where additional context could help the group navigate a choice.

You'll likely be surprised: many pencil sketches are 50-70% accurate to the final plan. But what matters most is how much better you'll be able to respond to conversation twists because you've already played through the possibilities.

Action Steps

- Block out quiet time to sketch your three-year plan
- Limit each year to three major goals max
- Think through dependencies, sequencing, and balance
- Use this draft only as a guide for facilitation

Chapter Review

- Pre-sketching helps you visualize how the plan fits together

- This exercise gives you strategic foresight—not control
- Most plans evolve during discussion, but your draft gives you a confident starting point
- The best facilitators prepare beyond the agenda—they anticipate the plan's shape before the room does

---

20

ALEX'S STORY: PREPARING

A lex had been thinking about the agenda all week. Not constantly, but in the background—while unloading the dishwasher, walking the dog, waiting in the pickup line at school. It hovered just under the surface, like a puzzle she hadn't quite solved yet.

She kept circling the same question: two hours or three and a half?

The shorter version was tempting. People liked short meetings. And technically, it could be enough time. But when she imagined the discussion—really pictured the conversations, the questions, the pauses for processing—it felt tight.

She'd caught herself halfway through drying dishes the night before, hands still damp, muttering, "Just look at it, Alex. You'll know."

So that morning, she sat down, opened the draft, and read through it with fresh eyes.

There were too many moving pieces for a two-hour sprint. Even if they trimmed a few goals, the rest still deserved time. Space. Breathing room.

She made her choice.

That afternoon, she called Shannon, the board president.

"Hey, I've got a draft of the agenda for the meeting. Want to take a look?"

Alex emailed the 3.5 hour version of the agenda. They reviewed it together over the phone. It was loose enough to allow for real conversation, but structured enough to guide them through the tough spots—alignment, disagreements, and finally, building out the plan.

"Are you leaning toward the 2-hour or 3.5-hour version?" Shannon asked.

Alex didn't hesitate. "Let's go with 3.5. We've got a solid number of goals to work through—even with six or so that are clearly off the table, there's still a lot to discuss. I want to give the group enough breathing room for real conversation without feeling rushed."

Shannon agreed. "That makes sense. Let's give it the space it needs. Plus no one will complain if we wrap up early. Send the email to the group tomorrow morning. Great work."

Approved. She exhaled.

The next morning, she opened a new message and typed:

Subject: Strategic Planning Meeting Packet + Agenda

Dear Team,

I'm excited to share our packet and agenda for the upcoming strategic planning meeting on September 15. Thank you again for the insight you contributed during our stakeholder survey and priority sort—it's helped shape a strong foundation for this next phase.

Attached you'll find:

An **agenda** that outlines our flow for the meeting

The **executive brief** capturing where BrightStart stands now

A **summary** of what we heard in the survey

A **visual analysis of goal priorities** across the group

A **blank planning grid** for your own notes as we build the plan together

We'll use this time to finalize our strategic direction and develop a shared plan for the next three years. If you have any questions ahead of time, feel free to reach out.

With appreciation, Alex

She hit send. Then, finally, leaned back in her chair, another major step completed.

It had been a full week. Between school pickups, laundry mountains, and juggling a dozen little work fires, Alex hadn't carved out much time to take a good look at how the goals may fit together or not.

But then Saturday morning brought an unexpected gift: a quiet hour. The kids were still asleep, the coffee was hot, and the house was calm. She tiptoed into the hallway, grabbed a stack of multi-colored sticky notes, and headed into her kids' hallway where the big whiteboard hung on the wall.

She erased drawings of dinosaurs and a chore list, and divided the space into three columns: Year 1, Year 2, Year 3. It wasn't glamorous, but it would work.

She opened her laptop and reviewed the heat map and draft goals. This part wasn't easy. Each decision felt connected to three others. Writing down each goal she started to categorize them by color. Red was governance, green had to do with fundraising, purple became programming goals, and yellow represented partnerships. She stuck "Improve volunteer onboarding" in Year 1 and immediately saw how it enabled the virtual mentoring program in Year 2. But where did "Launch literacy festival" fit? Could they really build that kind of event by Year 3 if the funding didn't solidify in Year 2?

Her coffee cooled as she moved notes back and forth, creating then scrapping sequences. There were too many goals for each year at first—six in Year 1, four in Year 2, five in Year 3. She forced herself to prioritize, to let some ideas go. The grid wasn't final, but it needed clarity.

Eventually, a loose shape emerged:

- Year One: Upgrade volunteer onboarding; deepen school partnerships; improve board-staff communication.
- Year Two: Launch virtual mentoring; strengthen evaluation tools; develop new funding partnerships.
- Year Three: Host literacy festival; expand programming to a new district; publish an annual community impact report.

She stood back and looked at the board.

If this played out, it would be transformational. More kids reading. More families involved. A board that didn't just meet —but led. And a community that saw BrightStart not just as helpful, but essential.

Her daughter padded into the hallway, still in pajamas, and gave the board a curious glance.

"Is that for work?" she asked.

Alex smiled. "Yep. Planning out something big."

"Looks like it," her daughter said, pointing to a sticky note. "That one should go at the top. I like that color best."

Alex laughed. "I'll think about it love."

She snapped a photo of the board with her phone, gathered the notes, and headed to her desk. She'd transfer this draft into her meeting binder later. For now, the fog had lifted. The logic puzzle made more sense. And she could see the path ahead.

21

FACILITATING THE STRATEGIC PLANNING MEETING

F acilitation is both an art and a skill—and this chapter is your mini masterclass. Whether you're a seasoned leader or new to guiding group discussion, it helps to have a few tools in your back pocket. Not because you expect things to go wrong, but because good facilitators know how to adapt when conversations go sideways, energy dips, or discussions get too deep into the weeds.

This chapter isn't about rigid rules. It's about anchoring you in confidence and clarity, so you can read the room, shift gears when needed, and still guide the group toward a shared outcome.

You don't need to be charismatic or extroverted to be effective. You just need to be present, prepared, and willing to trust the process you've built.

Let's walk through what it looks like to facilitate with confidence, even when the conversation gets complex or emotions run high.

Start with the Right Mindset

You're walking into this meeting with more clarity than most facilitators ever have:

- You know where there's alignment
- You've identified areas of disagreement
- You've drafted a possible layout for your strategic plan

That insight gives you a huge advantage. Your job is to hold space, guide discussion, and help the group build consensus. Not to push a particular agenda.

If You're the Executive Director, Too

If you're both facilitating and responsible for carrying out the plan, it can feel tricky. But you're not alone—many nonprofit leaders wear both hats. Here's how to do it well:

- **Step back strategically:** Prioritize guiding the process. Let others share ideas before you weigh in.
- **Clarify your role early:** Let your board know ahead of time that you'll be facilitating—not steering but will still weigh in when appropriate.

You don't have to carry both roles perfectly. You just need to show up with clarity and care.

_____

Navigating Group Dynamics

Every group has a mix of personalities. Your job isn't to fix that—it's to channel it.

- **For the talkers:** "Thanks for that insight, Carlos. I'd love to hear from someone who hasn't spoken yet."
- **For the quiet contributors:** "Jasmine, you've worked on similar projects—what do you see here?"
- **For the detail-oriented:** "Let's make a note of that detail for later. Right now, we're looking at big-picture placement."
- **For the skeptics:** "That's a good flag. How can we shape this goal to address your concern without losing momentum?"

You're not managing people—you're making space.

When You Hit a Disagreement

This is where your priority sort analysis becomes your best friend.

Instead of, "What does everyone think about this?" try:

"Our survey showed a split on this goal—some rated it high priority, others rated it low. Let's hear a few perspectives before we place it."

Questions to guide disagreement:

- "What would success look like if we pursued this?"

- "What would it take—time, money, people?"
- "How does it connect to our mission?"
- "What happens if we don't do it?"

Then ask: "Where should this go—high, medium, or set it aside?"

Aim for Consensus (Not Unanimity)

You don't need full agreement on every goal. You need enough agreement to move forward together.

Consensus often sounds like: "It's not my top priority, but I'm okay with it being in the plan."

That's progress.

———————————

Building the Plan Together

This part should feel collaborative and energizing.

Project your three-year planning grid. Start filling it in live.

- Begin with the easy wins. "It seems like everyone agrees this should go in Year One."
- Explore sequencing. "If this is in Year Two, what needs to happen first?"
- Balance effort. "We have four goals in Year One and only one in Year Three—how can we smooth that out?"

This visual, shared process helps the group feel like co-creators.

Common Challenges (and How to Respond)

- **"We're trying to do too much"**: Ask, "Which three goals would have the biggest impact if we focused there first?"
- **"This is too vague"**: Say, "Agreed—it needs clarity. But for now, does the general direction feel right?"
- **"We don't have resources"**: Ask, "What would need to be true to make this possible? Could we phase it or partner up?"
- **New ideas appear mid-meeting**: Say, "That's a great idea. Let's note it, and once we've finished the plan based on the survey, we can revisit new ideas."

Keeping Energy Up

This process takes focus. And it can drain energy fast.

- Take a short break every hour
- Redirect when conversations spiral into implementation: "These are great logistics—let's first agree it belongs in the plan."
- Celebrate progress out loud: "Look at what we've built already—Year One is agreed upon. That's huge."

The Magic Moment

There's always a shift—the moment people stop talking about goals and start talking about the future.

Someone will say, "This feels like exactly where we should be going."

That's your sign: they're not just agreeing on goals. They're building shared vision.

———————————

Wrapping Up Well

In your final 15–20 minutes:

- Review each year of the plan aloud
- Confirm understanding and alignment
- Clarify who's taking the first step on each major goal
- Share what comes next: follow-up meetings, reporting timelines, and how action plans will be built

Your final question: "Does this feel like the right framework for the next three years?"

If you get nods, you're there.

———————————

Action Steps

- Step into your role as facilitator—not the driver of content
- Guide discussion through alignment, disagreement, and decision
- Use your planning grid to build the plan live with your group
- Help the team sort priorities clearly and collaboratively
- Keep energy high with structure, breaks, and celebration

Chapter Review

- Facilitation is about making space—not controlling outcomes
- Your role is to guide, clarify, and hold structure steady
- Real-time building creates buy-in and momentum
- Consensus is more powerful than perfection
- A strong meeting ends with shared vision and next steps

22

CAPTURING DECISIONS IN THE ROOM

This chapter is your hands-on guide to capturing the right goals, in the right order, during your strategic planning meeting. You'll use a simple planning grid projected on-screen or printed for all to see. This is the tool you'll use to co-create your draft strategic plan in real time.

Your goal isn't to write everything down. It's to document clear agreements, goal placements, and initial responsibility so that you walk out with a shared, usable framework.

This chapter will show you how to:

- Know when a goal is ready to go on the plan
- Decide where it fits in the timeline
- Clarify who is initially responsible for next steps
- Keep the plan focused on outcomes, not details

What Is the Goal Grid?

The goal grid is a simple three-column layout labeled Year 1, Year 2, and Year 3. As the conversation unfolds, you'll add only the goals that the group agrees should be part of the plan. It's a shared visual of alignment in action.

STRATEGIC PLANNING
GOAL GRID EXAMPLE

Proposed Goal	Year One	Year Two	Year Three

When to Add a Goal

Only add a goal to the grid when the group agrees:

- It should be part of the three-year plan
- It belongs in a specific year based on readiness or dependencies
- Someone has agreed to take initial responsibility

Avoid listing goals "just to consider." This grid is for commitments, not brainstorming.

You can prompt placement with questions like:

"Is this a year one priority or something that builds later?"

"What would need to be true before we take this on?"

"Is this foundational to other goals?"

Who Owns What

Once a goal is placed, ask: "Who will take the lead on defining the path forward?"

This doesn't mean they'll do all the work. It means they'll:

- Draft the action plan after the meeting
- Define success indicators
- Report back on progress

Ownership could fall to an individual or a committee—either works. What matters most is that the person or group taking responsibility has enough knowledge and context to develop a realistic, effective action plan. They are closest to the implementation. They know what's possible, what barriers may exist, and what success looks like from the ground.

Assigning ownership keeps your plan alive. Without it, even the clearest plan fades from memory.

———————

This Is Not Implementation

You may hear: "We need to define this more clearly."

Pause and explain: "This meeting is about agreement and alignment. The person or team assigned will define the details."

The goal of the strategic planning meeting is to define the comprehensive plan—what goals belong, in which year, and who will lead each one. It's not about developing detailed action steps or success metrics in real time.

There's wisdom in waiting. The people responsible for leading the work are also the best suited to define what success looks like and how to get there. They understand the context, resources, and realities better than anyone else in the room.

To keep alignment intact, those assigned to each goal will report back to the board at least quarterly. These check-ins ensure that implementation stays connected to the vision and values established during the planning process.

Think of your planning group as setting the destination. The team or person assigned to a goal figures out the route—and keeps you updated along the way.

Keep It Focused

Your goal grid should:

- Include only goals the group has agreed on
- Avoid repeating background or process notes
- Keep phrasing concise
- Note who owns each goal

_____

After the Meeting

Take your working grid and clean it up. Use it to create the official one-page plan.

Send a draft to your participants within 48 hours with a quick note:

POST–MEETING EMAIL

Subject: Final Draft of Strategic Plan + What's Next

Hi everyone,

Thank you again for your time, insights, and thoughtful participation in our recent strategic planning process. I'm excited to share that the final draft of our Strategic Plan is now complete and attached.

This plan reflects the goals and agreements we made together during the meeting, and it represents a clear, aligned vision for our next three years.

Next Step: One-Page Action Plans To bring each of our Year One goals to life, we'll be working with the lead person or committee assigned to each goal to develop a short, one-page action plan.

These action plans will outline:

• Key milestones

• Timeline

• Success indicators

• Resources or support needed

Either I (or [insert name, e.g., our Executive Director or Board President]) will meet with each lead over the next few weeks to offer support and answer any questions as you draft your plan. These action plans will be reviewed by the board at our next regular board meeting to ensure alignment and offer any final guidance.

If you've been assigned to lead or support a goal, I'll be reaching out shortly to schedule a time to connect. If you have any questions in the meantime, feel free to reach out.

Thank you again for helping shape such a strong and thoughtful plan.

Thanks,

[Your Name]

Action Steps

- Use the goal grid during the meeting to document aligned goals
- Only add goals that have agreement, placement, and ownership
- Clarify who will define each goal's details and success
- Clean up the grid post-meeting to build your one-page plan

Chapter Review

- The goal grid is a tool for clarity, not complexity
- Agreement, timing, and ownership are your placement criteria
- Implementation begins after the meeting, by the people closest to the work
- Your meeting doesn't end with discussion—it ends with a shared direction

23

ALEX'S STORY: MEETING

Alex arrived 30 minutes early, latte in hand and nerves quietly buzzing beneath the surface. The meeting space was one of the brighter, warmer rooms in the library—soft carpet underfoot, natural light pouring through high windows, and the faint smell of fresh coffee drifting from a side table.

Shannon had picked up breakfast burritos from a local café and brought them in herself, along with a box of donuts, a fruit tray, and a carafe of strong coffee. Someone had even remembered oat milk. It felt intentional, welcoming. Like a team ready to do real work—together.

Folded chairs circled a long table. A bowl of peppermints sat in the center, next to a pitcher of water beading with condensation.

She took a deep breath and got to work.

Packets first. She laid one at each place as she moved around the table. Her own facilitator binder sat nearby, tabs crisp, sticky notes poking out as reminders. She connected her laptop to the projector—thankfully, no tech issues—and the blank planning grid glowed to life on the screen.

The room began to fill slowly. Voices warmed the space. Shannon greeted her with a reassuring smile and a quiet, "Looks great in here."

Alex nodded, managing a smile in return. Her palms were slightly damp. She tucked them behind her back.

––––––––––

"Thank you for being here," Alex said once everyone had settled. "Today is about building the strategic plan—together."

She gave a brief process review, walking them through the survey response rates, the priority sort, the heat map. There was something powerful in showing the group just how aligned they already were.

"You've each got a blank planning grid in your packets," she said, holding hers up. "As we talk through the goals, feel free to jot down where you think they belong. I'll be filling in our shared grid up here."

Heads nodded. Not many questions yet. The group was quiet, attentive. Some leaned in, pens ready but unmoving. There was a kind of focused anticipation in the air.

The first few goals were easy. Green-zone goals—clear agreement from the group. Alex projected the first one and read it aloud.

"Do we feel good about putting this in Year One?"

Quick nods. A few soft affirmations.

"That aligns with what we've been hearing," someone offered. Another chimed in, "It's already in motion—it just needs formal placement."

Alex smiled and dragged the goal into the Year One column. "Any objections to assigning this to the Program Committee to lead?"

A few glances around the table. Then someone said, "We're happy to take it."

It was working.

Three more goals followed, stacking neatly under Year One. But a tension was quietly building.

Alex could feel it—the subtle shift in the room. She glanced at the screen. Year One was starting to overflow.

One board member raised a hand, brow furrowed. "What's the right number of goals we can reasonably accomplish in a single year? We're loading a lot into Year One."

Alex nodded. "Great question. Let's flag this for now and revisit once we've worked through more of the list. From my research it looks like organizations can best be successful with three major goals per year. We can rebalance once we have the full picture."

Then came the first yellow-zone goal. Mixed support. Half the group had marked it high priority. The other half had left it blank.

Alex read the goal aloud: "Pilot a monthly family story-time in partnership with the community center."

A pause.

"I love the idea," one board member said. "But we've struggled to recruit volunteers for Saturday events."

Another chimed in: "But that's why we need this. We keep saying we want to reach more families, especially those who don't come to school-based events. This does that."

The conversation shifted. Not hostile—but layered. Real.

Alex let it play for a few minutes, listening closely. Then she flipped to a page in her binder.

"Here's something that came up in three separate survey comments," she said, reading from a printed page. "'We need to meet families where they are—not just during school hours.'"

There was a pause. Then a thoughtful nod from one of the skeptics.

"Okay," she said. "That helps. Maybe we try a limited version. Pilot it quarterly instead of monthly."

Alex adjusted the wording and left the goal in Year Two. Consensus—not perfect, but enough to move forward.

Then came the first red-zone (broad disagreement) goal: "Expand programming to include financial literacy workshops for parents."

"That's not what we're here to do," someone said, frowning. "This feels like mission drift."

Another replied, "But if we help parents build skills, that supports the whole family. And that can improve literacy outcomes, right?"

The room was quiet. The kind of quiet where people aren't sure if they should weigh in.

Alex flipped open her binder and turned to the first tab. "Let's take a moment to revisit our mission."

She read aloud: "BrightStart Readers exists to support early childhood literacy by connecting young readers with caring volunteers and evidence-based reading strategies."

Shannon added. "That mission is clear. Our focus is on early childhood literacy. Not general family services - that would dilute our focus."

There were a few murmurs of agreement. Someone added, "I like the intention behind the idea, but I don't think it belongs in this plan."

Alex nodded. "We can document the idea in the appendix for future exploration, but for now, we'll set it aside."

She moved on, and the group settled back into rhythm.

Alex jotted it in the notes section in her meeting packet.

As they progressed, they returned to the overstuffed Year One column. It was visibly lopsided.

Alex clicked to a new view.

"Let's look at the full grid again. Year One has five major goals. Year Two only has two. Year Three has four. What's realistic here?"

The group leaned in. One person said, "We can't launch all of these right away."

Someone else suggested, "What if we combine the onboarding update and the volunteer training refresh? They're closely linked."

Alex raised an eyebrow. "Would that keep the scope manageable?"

"Actually, yes," said the committee lead. "We'd just need to structure it carefully."

Two goals became one.

Another board member pointed to the Year Two column. "If we move the new mentor recruitment goal to Year Two, that gives us time to redesign the onboarding first. It's a dependency."

Alex nodded. "That's a good point. Let's think about what has to happen first to make other goals possible."

They started working backwards. One person proposed, "The community reading event shouldn't be in Year One. We don't have the partnerships yet. That belongs in Year Three."

Another added, "And to get there, we need that partnership outreach goal in Year Two. Otherwise, it's premature."

Slowly, the group began to move pieces like puzzle parts. Goals were shifted, some combined, others moved down the timeline.

Dependencies revealed themselves naturally: training before expansion, outreach before public events, evaluation before innovation.

As the board reshaped the plan, Alex quietly tracked their decisions on screen.

The grid began to balance—not just by number, but by logic.

As Alex typed in the final adjustments, she had a quiet realization: this plan, emerging line by line, wasn't far from the draft she'd sketched at home on the kids' whiteboard. Her early Saturday morning puzzle-solving had paid off. But what struck her now was how much better this version was— how real discussion had revealed overlooked dependencies, raised new questions, and led to smarter sequencing.

That little draft on the whiteboard had been her mental rehearsal. But this—this was the real thing, strengthened by many perspectives.

It felt like clarity.

They reached the final goal with six minutes to spare.

Three major goals per year. Each one assigned. No one looked exhausted. In fact, a few were still smiling.

"I'll clean up the formatting and send a draft Monday," Alex said. "But the structure—that's what we've built today. Together."

Shannon stood. "This is the most grounded, thoughtful planning meeting I've been part of in years. Thank you all. And thank you, Alex."

Applause. A few hugs. A sense of real, collective pride.

———————

That night, her family took her out to her favorite Thai restaurant. Candlelight flickered against the window. Her husband ordered appetizers before she could stop him. Her daughter handed her a crayon drawing that said, "You did it!"

Alex held the drawing and smiled, feeling the weight of the day settle into something softer. Her shoulders finally dropped. It wasn't just the relief of having gotten through it—it was the realization that she had done something meaningful, something lasting.

Over pad thai and jasmine tea, her son asked, "Did it go okay?"

Alex looked at him and nodded, her voice a little shaky from the emotion that was just catching up to her. "It went better than okay. It felt right."

That night, after bedtime stories and loading the dishwasher, she paused at her own kitchen counter. Binder still in her bag. But the plan—the real plan—was in her head, and more than that, in her heart.

She had planned. She had guided. And somehow, between the nerves and the notecards, she had led.

And together, they had built a plan worth following.

Alex felt something shift inside her—not just relief, but something bigger. A confidence she hadn't felt in a long time. This wasn't just about getting through a meeting. She had stepped into a new version of herself. One that could lead with calm, clarity, and heart.

She felt empowered and excited in a new way about her role with the organization. No longer just reacting to daily fires or pushing projects uphill. She now saw the arc of where they were going—and knew she could help shape it.

The meeting had ended hours ago, but the momentum still buzzed in her chest. Not the kind of adrenaline that fades, but the steady hum of belief. She had found her stride. And more than that, she'd found joy in the work.

24

BRINGING YOUR PLAN TO LIFE

Y ou did it.

You facilitated the conversation. You navigated the data, the dynamics, and the delicate moments. You helped your organization build a strategic plan that's clear, focused, and honest.

Now, here's the best part: the real change begins.

This chapter is about everything that comes after the planning meeting—what it looks like to actually bring your plan to life.

Not in theory. In real, everyday practice.

Because while the planning session may have been a moment of alignment and shared purpose, implementation is where that purpose becomes progress. It's where the goals you mapped out begin to take root in the daily rhythm of your organization.

And the good news?

You don't need to be perfect. You don't need to control every detail. You just need a steady structure that helps you stay focused on what matters most.

This chapter will show you how to build that structure.

With a few simple systems, regular check-ins, and a bit of celebration along the way, your one-page plan can become the most powerful tool in your organization—not because it's fancy, but because it actually gets used.

The Implementation Mindset

Your organization's plan isn't just a to-do list—it's a compass. It gives direction, not detailed marching orders. Strategic implementation means staying focused on your top priorities while remaining flexible when things change.

The leadership's role now is to keep that compass visible and gently reorient the organization to it—again and again.

Developing Year-One Action Plans

The strategic plan gave you the what. Now it's time to map the how.

As soon as your plan is finalized, your attention shifts to activation. That means supporting the individuals and committees who will lead each Year One goal as they translate strategy into actionable steps. Within 30 days of your planning meeting, either you or the executive director or board president should meet with each goal lead to help them outline a simple one-page action plan.

This is not a solo effort. Goal owners may pull in additional volunteers, subcommittees, or partners to help. But the first step is focus: aligning around the intended outcome and identifying a practical roadmap.

Each one-page action plan will be reviewed by the board to ensure strategic alignment and clarity. This structure keeps everyone rowing in the same direction, without requiring constant oversight.

Here's what each one should include:

ACTION PLAN EXAMPLE

Goal Statement: *Restate the strategic goal clearly.*

Success Indicator: *What does success look like?*

Milestones: *Three to five key steps or phases to accomplish the goal.*

Timeline: *Estimated dates for each milestone.*

Resources Needed: *Budget, staff, tools, or support.*

Responsible Party: *Committee or individual who owns the work.*

Support Needed from Leadership: *Any specific decisions, access, or coordination required.*

Progress Reporting Plan: *When and how updates will be shared with the board.*

Keep it short. One page is enough to clarify direction and allow for board oversight without micromanaging the details.

Action Plan Template Example

Strategic Goal: Redesign volunteer onboarding process.

Success Indicator: By Q4, 100% of new volunteers complete onboarding within 30 days of joining the organization.

Milestones:

- Survey recent volunteers about onboarding experience – Due: Feb 15 – Lead: Volunteer Committee

- Draft revised onboarding content – Due: Mar 15 – Lead: Claire, Committee Chair

- Pilot new process with spring volunteer cohort – Due: Apr 30 – Lead: Onboarding Subgroup

Resources Needed: Survey tool access, $250 for updated printed materials

Goal Owner: Volunteer Committee

Support from Leadership: Staff liaison to help coordinate content review

Progress Reporting: Updates at March and June board meetings

The Organization's Follow-Through System

Action plans are just the beginning. What brings your plan to life is consistent follow-through—ongoing touch-points that keep everyone aligned, supported, and moving forward. Here's how to structure that support across the organization.

Monthly Conversations with Goal Leads

Every goal has an owner—whether that's a person or a committee. Set up brief monthly chats (15–20 minutes is enough) or emails to check in, ask what they need, and listen. These aren't check-the-box meetings. They're about support, momentum, and relationship.

Quarterly Check-Ins

These are your anchor points. Schedule four strategic plan reviews per year—ideally right now, for the next 12 months. Keep them to 60–90 minutes.

This is where you:

- Review progress on each goal
- Troubleshoot roadblocks
- Adjust timelines if needed
- Celebrate what's been accomplished
- Remind everyone what matters most

Annual Review

Once a year, hold a deeper review session.

This is your moment to zoom out:

- What goals are complete?
- What needs to shift or roll forward?
- What have we learned?
- What should we do differently next year?

This process keeps the plan alive without overwhelming anyone.

Make the Plan Visible

Strategic plans fail when they disappear.

Post your organization's one-page plan somewhere visible—in the office, in staff break rooms, in board packets. Refer to it in staff and board meetings. Add a standing "Strategic Plan Update" line item to every board agenda—even if the update is just a sentence or two. You may want to add this year's goals to your organization's website.

The more people see it, the more they'll use it.

Archiving Your Work for the Future

One of the greatest gifts you can give to your future self—and to the next leader who steps into your role—is a clear, organized record of what was created.

Take time to compile a Strategic Planning Archive that includes:

- The finalized one-page strategic plan
- All approved one-page action plans (for each goal)
- Your facilitator packet and notes

- The executive brief and survey summaries
- The meeting agenda and participant list

Label it clearly and store both a printed version and a digital copy in a shared organizational folder. This archive becomes a legacy of alignment and clarity—something the next planning cycle can build upon, rather than start from scratch.

Celebrate Progress

You don't need confetti cannons. You just need to name wins in board meetings and/or in organizational newsletters:

"We completed Goal 1 ahead of schedule."

"That community event? It came from Goal 2 of our strategic plan."

Celebrating small wins builds momentum. It reminds people the plan isn't theoretical—it's real.

Handling Common Challenges

Sometimes the plan goes off track—and that's normal. Here's where leadership can play a key role in keeping the plan moving forward:

"We're behind schedule." *That's okay. Most plans fall behind at some point. Ask: Are we still moving in the right direction? What would help us move forward?*

"Priorities changed." *Revisit the plan quarterly. Adjust intentionally, not reactively.*

*"The team's losing energy."*Bring it back to purpose. Celebrate small wins. Make space to name frustrations and reset.

*"This new opportunity isn't in the plan."*Use your plan as a filter. If it supports a current goal—go for it. If not, ask: is it worth adjusting the plan, or just parking it for later?

Leadership can step in here—sometimes just asking the right question or giving a gentle reminder helps steer things back on course.

Make Implementation a Habit

This work gets easier the more you do it.

Train your team or organizational staff to ask: "How does this align with our strategic plan?"Use your plan to:

- Prioritize budget decisions
- Allocate staff time
- Weigh new opportunities
- Guide committee work

This turns your plan into a daily decision-making tool.

Planning Ahead

Six months before your current plan expires, begin gathering feedback:

- What worked well?
- What stalled?
- What do we want to carry forward into the next plan?

This way, your next planning cycle builds on real experience —not guesswork.

Your strategic plan is more than a document—it's a promise.

A promise to stay focused, to move forward together, and to lead with clarity.

By following through—not perfectly, but persistently—you're creating something rare and valuable: a plan that actually lives. One that adapts, inspires, and keeps your organization pointed toward what matters most.

This is the kind of leadership that builds trust. This is the kind of clarity that moves communities.

And you're the one who helped make it real. Congratulations!

25

ALEX'S STORY: BRINGING THE PLAN TO LIFE

A lex tucked a slim folder into her tote bag and zipped up her coat. The coffee shop was quiet this time of morning, the kind of quiet that invited real conversations. She had back-to-back meetings that day—each one with a board member who had stepped up to lead a strategic goal.

It had been three weeks since the planning meeting. The energy from that day still hummed in her chest, but now came the quieter part—the follow-through. The doing.

First up was Claire, head of the Volunteer Committee. They met at the corner table near the window, each with a notebook and a steaming mug of coffee. Claire opened their meeting with a smile. "I've already pulled together two volunteers to help map out the action plan for our onboarding redesign. We thought we could break it into three phases."

Alex nodded, encouraged. Claire pulled a blank worksheet from her notebook, already scribbled with early notes.

Together, they refined it into a simple one-page action plan—three milestones, a proposed timeline, and a list of needs. At the top, the goal was restated clearly. Below that, each milestone had a brief description, a target completion date, and a note about who was responsible. There was even a short line about what success would look like.

Nothing fancy. But solid. Focused. Achievable.

Alex reminded her gently, "The board will be reviewing each goal's action plan—so it doesn't need to be perfect, but it does need to be clear enough to guide your work and show progress."

Her next meeting, though, was different.

Jordan, the board lead for Community Partnerships, slid into the booth with a look of mild panic. "Alex, I need help. I've got the goal, but I'm not sure how to break it down. Everything feels... big."

Alex offered a reassuring smile and flipped open a blank action plan worksheet between them.

"Let's start simple. What would success look like for this goal?"

Jordan paused. "We'd have at least two new partnership agreements with local schools or libraries."

"Great," Alex said. "Let's call that the outcome. Now, what needs to happen to get there?"

Together, they unpacked the steps—identifying potential partners, drafting a partnership template, scheduling introductory meetings. By the end of the hour, they had a basic outline of three milestones, with target months and names next to each.

"That wasn't as bad as I thought," Jordan admitted, looking down at the finished plan.

"It always feels daunting at first," Alex said. "But you had all the details in your mind—we just worked together to get them onto paper."

Meeting after meeting, the pattern repeated. Program leads, fundraising chairs, even the facilities liaison. Each came with ideas. Some were polished. Some needed nurturing. But they all left with the same thing: clarity.

And more than that—they had ownership over their individual goal and had the background to make sure the action plans were realistic and achievable.

Three months later, the conference room buzzed with the low hum of side conversations and chair legs scraping against tile. It was their first quarterly strategic plan check-in. Alex sat in her chair with a printed agenda and a quiet sense of confidence she wouldn't have recognized a year ago.

One by one, the committee leads shared updates. Some were ahead of schedule. Some had hit snags. One team had discovered that their original timeline was too ambitious—but they'd adjusted course and found a new solution.

Alex took notes, nodded, and asked gentle, curious questions. "What helped you move so quickly on this?" "What's getting in the way?" "What kind of support would move this forward?"

They were honest. Not defensive. Not afraid. There was

laughter. A few grateful shoutouts. And more than one proud smile.

Toward the end of the meeting, Alex projected the one-page plan—the same grid they had created together.

She added a small checkmark next to the goals already in motion.

It wasn't perfect. But it was working.

She was watching the group—people who used to show up tired, hesitant, or distracted—now engaged, contributing, moving.

She had facilitated that. Not because she had all the answers, but because she had built a process that worked.

A plan they believed in. A structure that supported real progress. A space where momentum could build.

She gathered her binder and laptop as the room began to empty. Someone had brought muffins. The coffee was nearly gone. But the feeling in the room? That would stay with her.

This was strategic planning done right.

Clear. Collaborative. Courageous.

And as she walked out into the bright afternoon light, Alex felt something simple and steady rise within her:

Pride.

Not just in the plan—but in the leader she'd become.

Because she knew now: clarity isn't something you wait for. It's something you help create.

And she had done it.

So can you.